Building for Wellness
THE BUSINESS CASE

Project Director and Author
Anita Kramer

Primary Author
Terry Lassar

Contributing Authors
Mark Federman
Sara Hammerschmidt

This project was made possible in part through the generous financial support of ULI Foundation Governor Bruce Johnson.

ULI also wishes to acknowledge the Colorado Health Foundation for its support of the ULI Building Healthy Places Initiative.

Urban Land Institute
Building Healthy
Places Initiative

Urban Land Institute
ULI Center for Capital Markets
and Real Estate

ULI Foundation

Recommended bibliographic listing:
Kramer, Anita, Terry Lassar, Mark Federman, and Sara Hammer-schmidt. *Building for Wellness: The Business Case*. Washington, D.C.: Urban Land Institute, 2014.

ISBN: 978-0-87420-334-9

© 2014 Urban Land Institute
1025 Thomas Jefferson Street, NW
Suite 500 West
Washington, DC 20007-5201

ACRONYMS

HEPA—high-efficiency particulate absorption
HOA—homeowners association
HUD—U.S. Department of Housing and Urban Development
HVAC—heating, ventilation, and air conditioning
LEED—Leadership in Energy and Environmental Design
VOC—volatile organic compound

MEASUREMENTS

ac—acre
ha—hectare
km—kilometer
mi—mile
sq ft—square foot
sq m—square meter

About the Urban Land Institute

The mission of the Urban Land Institute is to provide leadership in the responsible use of land and in creating and sustaining thriving communities worldwide. ULI is committed to

- Bringing together leaders from across the fields of real estate and land use policy to exchange best practices and serve community needs;
- Fostering collaboration within and beyond ULI's membership through mentoring, dialogue, and problem solving;
- Exploring issues of urbanization, conservation, regeneration, land use, capital formation, and sustainable development;
- Advancing land use policies and design practices that respect the uniqueness of both the built and natural environments;
- Sharing knowledge through education, applied research, publishing, and electronic media; and

- Sustaining a diverse global network of local practice and advisory efforts that address current and future challenges.

Established in 1936, the Institute today has more than 30,000 members worldwide, representing the entire spectrum of the land use and development disciplines. Professionals represented include developers, builders, property owners, investors, architects, public officials, planners, real estate brokers, appraisers, attorneys, engineers, financiers, academics, students, and librarians.

ULI relies heavily on the experience of its members. It is through member involvement and information resources that ULI has been able to set standards of excellence in development practice. The Institute has long been recognized as one of the world's most respected and widely quoted sources of objective information on urban planning, growth, and development.

About the Building Healthy Places Initiative

The ULI Building Healthy Places Initiative is leveraging the power of ULI's global networks to shape projects and places in ways that improve the health of people and communities.

In January 2013, ULI's board of directors approved a focus on healthy communities as a cross-disciplinary theme for the organization. Through the Building Healthy Places Initiative, launched in July 2013, ULI is working to promote health in projects and places across the globe.

ULI is focusing on four main areas of impact:

- **Raising awareness.** Raise awareness of the connections between health and the built environment in the real estate community, and work to make sure health is a mainstream consideration.

- **Defining the approach.** Help to define and share information about the design elements, programming strategies, materials, and other approaches that improve health for people.
- **Exploring the value proposition.** Build understanding of the market and nonmarket factors at play in building healthy places, and the value proposition of building and operating in health-promoting ways.
- **Advancing the state of practice and policy.** Using the ULI membership as a lever, and in partnership with others, advance the state of policy and practice.

We invite you to learn more at www.uli.org/health.

About the ULI Center for Capital Markets and Real Estate

The ULI Center for Capital Markets and Real Estate focuses on tracking, analyzing and exploring real estate investment trends globally. The mission is to inform, educate, explore issues, create knowledge, and foster communication and networking at the intersection of real estate finance and capital markets and the diverse needs and interests of the ULI membership. The Center also seeks to address members' interests in underlying topics such as market forces affecting property sectors and economic trends.

AUTHORS

Project Director and Author
Anita Kramer

Primary Author
Terry Lassar

Contributing Authors
Mark Federman
Sara Hammerschmidt

ULI PROJECT STAFF

Anita Kramer
Vice President
ULI Center for Capital Markets and Real Estate

Mark Federman
Project Assistant, ULI Center for Capital Markets
and Real Estate

Sara Hammerschmidt
Associate, Content

Rachel MacCleery
Senior Vice President, Content

Dean Schwanke
Senior Vice President, Case Studies and Publications

James A. Mulligan
Senior Editor

David James Rose
Editor

Betsy VanBuskirk
Creative Director

Craig Chapman
Senior Director, Publishing Operations

ULI SENIOR EXECUTIVES

Patrick L. Phillips
Chief Executive Officer

Cheryl Cummins
Executive Officer

Michael Terseck
Chief Financial Officer/Chief Administrative Officer

Jason Ray
Chief Technology Officer

Lela Agnew
Executive Vice President, Communications

Kathleen B. Carey
Executive Vice President/Chief Content Officer

David Howard
Executive Vice President, Development and
ULI Foundation

Joe Montgomery
Chief Executive, Europe

John Fitzgerald
Chief Executive, Asia Pacific

Marilee Utter
Executive Vice President, District Councils

Contents

Executive Summary

DOES WELLNESS MAKE BUSINESS SENSE AS A DEVELOPMENT OBJECTIVE? How have developers pursued this objective? What has the market response been? And how have developers measured their success?

This publication provides answers directly from developers who have completed projects with wellness intentions. In 13 sets of interviews, developers explain their motivation, their intended wellness and health outcomes, the development process and operations as related to their health intentions, and the key issue in this publication—the metrics of market performance.

Each chapter focuses on an overall development strategy and showcases a variety of building products and sectors within each strategy:

✳ Chapter 1: Renovation/redevelopment
  • Apartment buildings (two)
  • Business/call center
  • Mixed-use building (apartments, office, and retail)
  • Fitness/wellness/primary care facility

FIGURE 1: OVERVIEW OF BUILDING FOR WELLNESS PROFILES

Chapter	Project name	Location	Use
1. RENOVATION/REDEVELOPMENT	Eco Modern Flats[1]	Fayetteville, AR	Apartments
	Innovation Park	Charlotte, NC	Business park (back office, call centers)
	1221 Broadway[1]	San Antonio, TX	Apartments
	Jackson Walk	Jackson, TN	Fitness/wellness/primary care center
	The Century Building[2]	Pittsburgh, PA	Mixed use: workforce and market-rate housing, office, retail
2. NEW CONSTRUCTION	Via6	Seattle, WA	Mixed use: apartments and retail
	The Interlace	Singapore	Condominiums
	Park 20|20	Haarlemmermeer, Netherlands	Office
	Via Verde[2,3]	New York, NY	Workforce co-ops, low-income apartments
3. MASTER-PLANNED COMMUNITIES	Grow Community	Bainbridge Island, WA	Single-family homes, apartments
	Selandra Rise	Casey, Australia	Single-family homes
	Rancho Sahuarita	Tucson, AZ	Single-family homes, retail
	Mueller	Austin, TX	Single-family and multifamily homes, retail, office

* Wellness features noted here are those discussed in chapters 1–3. Some projects may have additional or planned features.

1. Finalist, ULI Global Awards for Excellence, 2013.
2. Winner, ULI's Jack Kemp Excellence in Affordable and Workforce Housing Awards, 2012.
3. Winner, ULI Global Awards for Excellence, 2013.

✳ Chapter 2: New construction
- Apartment building
- Mixed use (apartments, retail)
- Condominium development
- Office building

✳ Chapter 3: Master-planned communities
- Intown
- Greenfield (three).

Ten of the projects are located in eight states in the United States, primarily in secondary or smaller markets. Two projects are in the Asia Pacific region (Singapore and Australia) and one is in the Netherlands.

Profiled projects were identified through the Urban Land Institute District Council and National Council network, the ULI Global Awards for Excellence program, ULI's Jack Kemp Excellence in Affordable and Workforce Housing Awards program, and ULI's Case Studies program, as well as through information collected at ULI's 2013 Fall Meeting and Building Healthy Places Conference in early 2014.

While the profiles acknowledge the advantages that particular locations offer, projects were chosen for the wellness features specifically developed on site.

Studies are underway at three of the projects to measure the specific health benefits of the wellness strategies implemented and inform future strategies. The focus of this publication is on the business case for projects with such wellness objectives as encouraging physical activity, improving the indoor environment, and encouraging social engagement.

Highlights

The following are the common themes among the 13 profiled projects:

✳ Market response—the metric most reported by the 13 developers—has exceeded developer expectations with rapid lease-up and sales rates, higher rents than pro forma projections, rent and

SUMMARY OF WELLNESS FEATURES, BY PROJECT AND INTENT*

Clean indoor air	General physical/ pedestrian activity through project design	Support for bicycling	Structured fitness activity through built amenities	Structured fitness/ wellness activity through programming	Natural lighting/ daylighting	Social interaction	Other
✓	✓		✓			✓	✓
	✓	✓	✓	✓			
	✓		✓	✓	✓	✓	
	✓		✓	✓			
✓			✓	✓			
		✓	✓			✓	
	✓		✓			✓	✓
✓	✓	✓	✓	✓	✓	✓	✓
✓	✓	✓	✓	✓		✓	
✓	✓	✓	✓			✓	
	✓	✓	✓	✓		✓	
	✓	✓	✓	✓		✓	
✓	✓	✓	✓	✓		✓	

> **"Our overall success indicates that the strategic positioning . . . through an amenities program that promotes health and wellness can differentiate a community . . . and mitigate long-term risks."**
>
> —Robert Sharpe, developer, Rancho Sahuarita

sales premiums, and waiting lists. New interest by lenders and investors is also noted.

✳ Development costs attributable to the inclusion of wellness components, where mentioned, were generally reported as a minimal percentage of the overall development budget. The notable exception is a highly amenitized master-planned community where these costs are partially offset by homebuilder and resale fees.

✳ There is a strong consensus that upfront development costs—even for those individual components that were significantly more costly than standard approaches—were well worth the cost and contributed to the projects' overall success. Challenges, such as working with contractors with little experience with nontraditional building systems, were noted as requiring additional time.

✳ Operating expenses for maintenance of wellness components, when noted, were typically minimal. Expenses, such as a full-time director of tenant services to market the wellness amenities at a business park or a full-time groundskeeper who also cultivates the community garden in an apartment complex, are noted as worth the investment. Operating and maintenance costs in master-planned communities are covered by the homeowners association fee.

✳ Programming—such as fitness classes, walking groups, wellness seminars, gardening classes, "walking school buses"—is used as a means to offer additional wellness opportunities as well as to encourage the use of wellness amenities.

✳ Partnerships with local nonprofit organizations, businesses, and jurisdictions are often formed to provide the programming. For example, at a business park, the local YMCA teaches on-site fitness classes and leads walking groups, while business tenants and local wellness professionals provide free seminars. In a master-planned community, a local health care provider offers a children's "Be Well" summer camp and "Walk with a Doc" programs.

✳ Social interaction is purposefully planned for and encouraged through the design of the project, choice and placement of amenities, and programming.

✳ Three of the projects—Selandra Rise, Mueller, and Park 20|20—are currently under study by universities and foundations regarding their impact on residents' and workers' health, well-being and productivity. Two university studies have previously concluded that Mueller residents had increased their physical activity by 40 to 50 minutes per week after moving in.

✳ Strategies used to build and provide for wellness can be grouped into seven categories of intent. As shown in figure 1, the number and combination of strategies used by each of the 13 projects vary, and the profiles themselves show the variety in the implementation of each strategy. (Figure 1 summarizes the information presented in each profile; it should be noted that some projects may have additional or planned features not profiled in this report.)

Wellness Strategies

The following list provides examples of strategies for each of the seven categories of intent:

✳ **Clean indoor air.** Nonsmoking policy, ductless heating/cooling, non-VOC materials, green walls.

✳ **General physical/pedestrian activity through project design.** Active staircase, interconnected network of sidewalks and trail system, car-free site, use of interconnected interior corridors for indoor track, shaded sidewalks, jogging track around perimeter of site that is wide enough to double as access for emergency vehicles.

* **Support for bicycling.** Protected bike lanes, multi-tool bike-repair station, private bicycle shop as project anchor, on-site bicycle commuter center, on-site bike-share program, bike storage facilities.

* **Structured fitness activity through built amenities.** Expansive fitness centers, fitness center in same building as preventative care/wellness center, themed gardens and trails, multiple fitness rooms with specialized equipment, rooftop/open-air workout space and exercise equipment, 50-meter pool.

* **Structured fitness/wellness activity through programming.** Fitness classes, walking groups, wellness seminars, runs/races, walking school buses.

* **Social interaction.** Community gardens, urban agriculture, greenhouses, design/themes of courtyards, a block party before first residents moved in allowing them to meet beforehand/form interest groups, classes on a range of interests that also promote social cohesion of the community.

* **Other intentions.** Chemical-free outdoors through use of native vegetation and a saltwater pool, natural light for office space through building design and LED lighting, aging-in-place condominium units, and universal design principles applied to fitness amenities.

The 13 projects that follow were chosen because they include a variety of wellness features and represent a range of project types, and because all of these developers consider their projects a business success. This group of projects does not necessarily represent the universe of such projects, so the observations and conclusions noted above are not necessarily universally applicable. However, it is hoped that the project details are educational and inspire further discussion and innovation.

ECO Modern Flats
Timothy Hursley

ECO Modern Flats
Fayetteville, Arkansas

PROJECT DATA

USE
MULTIFAMILY HOUSING
96 RENTAL UNITS

YEAR OPENED
2011

SITE SIZE
2.9 AC (1.2 HA)

RENTAL RATES
$795–$990 (INCLUDES UTILITIES,
INTERNET, CABLE)

PROJECT COST
$7.4 MILLION

DEVELOPER
SPECIALIZED REAL ESTATE
GROUP

OWNERS
ROBERT DANT, SPECIALIZED
REAL ESTATE GROUP

ARCHITECT/LANDSCAPE DESIGNER
MODUS STUDIO

LENDERS
CONSTRUCTION: USBANK;
PERMANENT: GRANDBRIDGE
REAL ESTATE GROUP

EQUITY PARTNER
ROBERT DANT

THE FAYETTEVILLE APARTMENT MARKET had long been dominated by a single developer who built mostly on large suburban tracts. But Specialized Real Estate Group, formerly a property management firm, recognized a significant market of young professionals and students looking for a rental product unavailable in the city: urban apartments with high-end design and premium amenities. In addition, "creating a built environment that promotes sustainability and good health was especially important to me," says Jeremy Hudson, CEO of Specialized. "I grew up with severe allergies and asthma, and it wasn't until much later that I learned how much our living conditions affect our health."

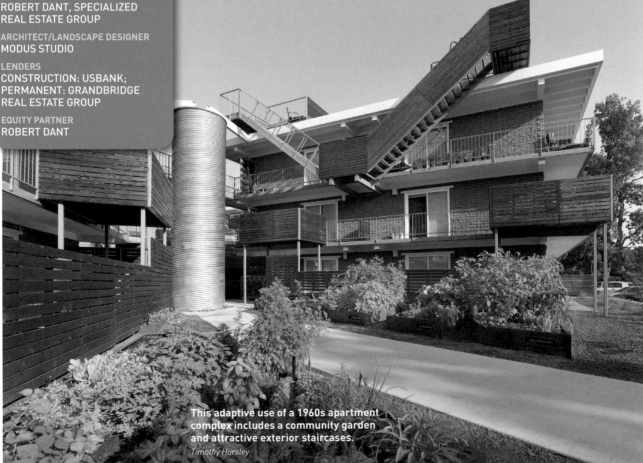

This adaptive use of a 1960s apartment complex includes a community garden and attractive exterior staircases.
Timothy Hursley

ECO Modern Flats, a rehab of a 1960s apartment complex, was the first development in the state to promote health and the state's first multifamily complex to be LEED certified, achieving a Platinum rating. The group of four buildings includes 96 one-bedroom apartments, each 600 square feet (56 sq m), and is located adjacent to the University of Arkansas and downtown Fayetteville. ECO Modern Flats has a Walk Score (from www.walkscore.com) of 85, indicating it is "very walkable."

Main Wellness Features

CLEAN INDOOR AIR

Strategies. A wide array of strategies were used to provide high-quality indoor air:

* A nonsmoking policy, strictly enforced, both indoors and outside. Eco Modern Flats is the first and only completely nonsmoking apartment complex in the region. According to the developer, this policy attracted more residents than it turned away, and this success has encouraged Specialized to make its other apartment complexes under construction nonsmoking as well.
* BioBased spray foam insulation, which is GreenGuard certified, representing independent verification of good indoor air quality attributes.

* Non-VOC paints, stains, and finishes, used throughout the complex, that emit no harmful gases and chemicals; some of these materials follow LEED guidelines that address indoor air quality.
* A ductless, energy-efficient, mini-split heating and cooling system to reduce the amount of mildew, mold, and dust that collects compared with a traditional HVAC system.
* A roller-shade window covering made of synthetic material that emits no VOCs.
* Kitchen countertops made of poured concrete, eliminating use of traditional chemical-based sealants.
* Concrete floors. The developer took advantage of the structure's original concrete material for flooring throughout the new development. In addition to creating an interesting aesthetic, the floors eliminate use of toxic glue and formaldehyde frequently found in carpets. The hard, smooth surfaces also are less likely to harbor dust mites and other allergens.

Development. Though the healthy building components did not increase engineering or design fees, the developer found it challenging to work with those contractors who had no experience with healthier materials and nontraditional building

Concrete flooring, non-VOC finishes, and a ductless heating and cooling system are a few of the strategies used to provide clean indoor air.
Adaptive Creative

Before and after images show how the buildings were adapted to create a well-designed and healthy apartment complex, including a central saltwater pool.
Timothy Hursley (top)
Adaptive Creative (bottom)

systems. "Anytime you ask a contractor to do something they're not accustomed to, there's a learning curve, and you're going to pay a premium," Hudson says. Measures to achieve cleaner indoor air were part of a larger holistic approach that included aggressive strategies to reduce energy use, ultimately halving the development's utility costs, he notes.

The overall premium for purchasing materials and equipment to improve indoor air quality was less than 1.5 percent of the overall development budget, the developer estimates; the new materials and equipment also improved energy efficiency. Because non-VOC paint and stains are readily available, additional costs associated with their use over conventional materials were minimal. However, the concrete countertops cost about twice

as much as traditional laminate, and the ductless heating system cost about 10 percent more than a traditional system.

Maintenance. The ductless heating and cooling system requires additional preventative maintenance; in particular, Specialized cleans the HEPA filters every three months. Although the concrete features require special maintenance procedures—Specialized rewaxes the concrete kitchen countertops every six months—the added durability of the concrete floors and countertops compared with traditional materials makes up for the minimal additional maintenance expense. Concrete floors eliminate the expense of regular carpet replacement. The developer also educates residents about appropriate cleaning products for upkeep.

As an alternative to concrete floors, which are too costly for new construction, Specialized is installing chemical-free vinyl synthetic flooring in its new developments; this flooring has the benefits of being allergen-free and durable like concrete but costs less.

CHEMICAL-FREE OUTDOORS

The use of chemicals outside was minimized through the following strategies:
* Native, drought-tolerant plants and noninvasive species planted on the grounds.
* An outdoor swimming pool filled with saltwater, which is more comfortable for swimmers and

healthier than the heavily chlorinated water it replaced. Although slightly higher upfront investment was needed, the annual operating costs for operating a saltwater pool are similar to those for chlorinated systems. Specialized is switching to saltwater pools for other apartment developments in its portfolio.

COMMUNITY GARDEN/SOCIAL INTERACTION

No other apartment complex in the area offered a community garden. The developer believes the 350-square-foot (33 sq m) garden, in a series of raised planters, was an important amenity to help attract its target market—young renters interested in gardening and easy access to healthy foods. Located next to the pool courtyard and barbecue area, the garden promotes social interaction and serves as the heart of the residential complex and a popular gathering place.

Specialized met with the first ECO residents to determine how to manage the garden. Many community gardens are divided into separate plots and maintained individually. However, the developer learned that, although most of the 20-something residents were interested in healthy foods and access to fresh produce, they did not want the responsibility of maintaining their own garden plots. In response, the developer built a shared community garden. A few residents who prefer to plant their own gardens were given small parcels.

The cost of maintaining the garden runs about 25 percent of total landscaping costs and 1.25 percent of the project's overall operating budget. Specialized employs a full-time groundskeeper to maintain the site's landscaping, including the garden; once a year, Specialized collects information from residents about specific herbs and vegetables they want in the garden. "If we could encourage more of our residents to care for their own gardens, we could reduce maintenance costs," says Hudson. But he views the $6,000 or so that Specialized spends on maintaining the garden as well worth the investment. The garden's success has prompted Specialized to include similar amenities in its other multifamily developments.

Performance

Since its completion in January 2011, ECO has been fully leased and has a waiting list. Current rents run 113 to 140 percent of pro forma estimates, significantly higher than those for comparable apartments in the area. Rent rates of $1.42 per square foot are higher than the average of 99 cents per square foot for comparable one-bedroom units in the area. Since the project opened, turnover has been about 15 percent lower than the market average.

"ECO confirmed our belief that there was a significant market of potential renters who were not being served," Hudson says. "These renters-by-choice were interested in urban-style apartments with modern design, premium amenities, as well as green and healthy building features"; they were also willing to pay a premium even for apartments significantly smaller (15 to 20 percent) than the norm.

ECO was Specialized's first significant development project. Its market success encouraged investors to team up with Specialized on a number of additional new multifamily developments in the area and emboldened other development firms to build apartments in the city on infill sites.

Several features of the complex promote social interaction, including a community garden, pool, courtyard, and rooftop deck.
Timothy Hursley

Innovation Park
Charlotte, North Carolina

PROJECT DATA

USE
BUSINESS PARK
1.9 MILLION SQ FT (82,000 SQ M)
OFFICE

YEAR OPENED
2010

SITE SIZE
200 AC (80 HA)

LEASE RATES
$21.50–$23.00 PER SQ FT, FULL
SERVICE

PROJECT COST
$77 MILLION

DEVELOPER/OWNER
BECO SOUTH LLC

ARCHITECT
REDLINE DESIGN GROUP

FINANCING
FINANCED ENTIRELY WITH
DEVELOPER EQUITY

WHEN CHRIS EPSTEIN, NOW HEAD OF BECO SOUTH, first visited the nearly empty 2 million-square-foot (186,000 sq m) former IBM complex in the University City neighborhood of Charlotte as head of leasing for BECO Management, he envisioned a turnaround strategy for reviving the moribund campus. Having read about Google's multiple-building complex in Mountain View, California, and its array of attractive amenities, Epstein set as the core of his strategy to "Google-ize" the Charlotte campus, offering high-quality fitness and health amenities not typically found in suburban multitenant buildings and scarcely associated with call centers and other back-office operations.

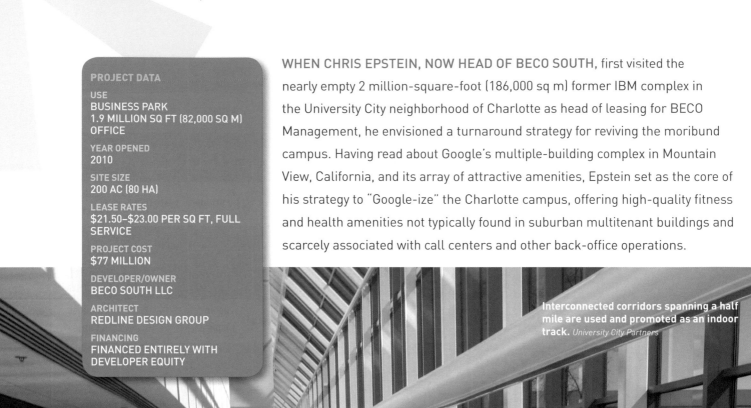

Interconnected corridors spanning a half mile are used and promoted as an indoor track. *University City Partners*

Several developers had attempted to redevelop the site. When BECO Management, which specializes in purchasing and turning around distressed real estate, first learned about the 200-acre (80 ha) site, the property was in receivership. BECO purchased the campus—which had a 70 percent vacancy rate—in 2010 for $42 million in cash, and Epstein relocated from Washington, D.C., to head BECO South, a new division to be led from Charlotte. Using its own resources, BECO spent $35 million cash renovating the campus, as well as adding 2,300 parking spaces and Google-style amenities in an effort to reposition the campus as an office park for call centers and back-office users.

Epstein views himself as an "evangelist" of work/life balance and well-being; a primary goal is "giving people the opportunity to make healthy choices," he says. Additional amenities at Innovation Park are charging stations for electric cars, subsidized daycare, a dry cleaner, a farmers market, multiple on-site food options, and wifi-enabled indoor and outdoor brainstorming spaces.

Main Wellness Features

Epstein estimates that about 2 percent of his development budget was spent on wellness components.

FITNESS CENTER

The $1 million, 7,000-square-foot (650 sq m) fitness center offers a wide array of cardiovascular equipment, plus individual audio-visual stations, strength-building systems, and group fitness classes that include Zumba, Pilates, yoga, and strength training. Members are charged $99 per year. "We could have made the center free, but we wanted people to have some skin in the game so that they would be more likely to actually use the facility," says Epstein. BECO South partners with the local YMCA, which teaches two fitness classes per day, at lunch and in the evening. Members can also participate in the YMCA Stay Healthy Fitness Challenge, an eight-week program promoting health and wellness in which participants are evaluated at the start and end of the program to assess their progress.

The center, which remains open until 10 p.m., is operating near capacity, and BECO South is planning to build a second one soon to accommodate the influx of new tenants. "In contrast to most office gyms, which are typically cramped, closet-like

The centrally located fitness center is a big draw for prospective tenants.
Rebecca Shrum

The local Y organizes walking groups through the campus for employees.
University City Partners

spaces, BECO Fitness was designed to resemble a high-end Equinox-style facility," says leasing director Mercedes Merritt. The fitness center has played a critical role in the lease-up of the project, Merritt says, describing the "a-ha" moment prospective tenants experience when they first see the center. Moreover, tenants like the notion of shifting the cost of pricey amenities like the fitness center onto their landlord. According to the developer, the fitness center grosses about $80,000 a year, but BECO South breaks even on the facility after paying a fee to the Y to manage the classes, plus depreciation of equipment.

FITNESS AND WELLNESS PROGRAMMING

The developer has implemented a number of programs to promote physical exercise and wellness, including a bike-sharing program. Initially, the bikes were scarcely used; once the developer introduced programming and marketing to call attention to the 25 free bikes on campus, enrollment soared. BECO South contracted with the Y to bring in a trainer to lead orientation sessions and bike tours. "It's not enough just to place bikes on campus and expect that people will use them," says Merritt. "It's all about marketing the message."

The project employs a full-time director of tenant services specifically to market the amenities.

To call attention to the bike-sharing program, tenant services director Rebecca Shrum suspended a bike from the ceiling in an office corridor with an E.T. figure peeking out of its basket. She also placed signs throughout the complex encouraging workers to complete their waiver to ride a bike, and "grab your helmet and go." Shrum spends about 40 percent of her time on programming for the health and fitness amenities.

BECO South also promotes the half mile (0.8 km) of interconnected corridors at the 13-building complex as an indoor track and contracted with the Y to organize walking groups for employees. The developer also partners with a tenant—a chiropractor/massage practice—to organize monthly wellness seminars. The first seminar, "Get Fit while You Sit," specifically addressed call center workers, who rarely leave their desks during the day. The second session, "Your Body Is Talking: 10 Reasons Why You Should Listen," was equally successful. The seminars are free and open to all employees of park businesses.

Innovation Park holds annual health fairs. BECO South started out working with a local hospital to

check key health statistics—such as cholesterol levels and blood pressure—but moved to a model that instead focuses more on prevention and holistic approaches to encourage a healthy lifestyle. BECO South brings in life coaches, nutritionists, chiropractors, and other alternative health care professionals who meet with employees during a two-hour lunch session. Local vendors were selected for the program in order to give them exposure and help them expand their businesses.

Performance

It has been nearly four years since the developer first imagined the vision for Innovation Park. As of June 2013, the campus is 93 percent leased. Nearly 5,000 employees currently work on campus, and an additional 1,600 employees from Allstate will be relocating there starting in April 2014. Additional large new tenants that joined the campus since BECO South purchased it include Wells Fargo & Co., AXA Equitable, and Siemens; in August 2013, Areva moved its North American headquarters here. The developer has just closed on its first 40,000-square-foot (3,600 sq m) stand-alone, built-to-suit building on the campus. Epstein was espe-

cially pleased with the outcome of the project when AXA Equitable asked to participate in placing $100 million in permanent financing on the project. "AXA Equitable is a tenant and now also our lender at Innovation Park; that is a very powerful endorsement of the project's transformation," Epstein says. He speculates that the complex is now worth close to $200 million, not including the undeveloped land.

Employees take advantage of the complex's bike-sharing program.
University City Partners

1221 Broadway
San Antonio, Texas

PROJECT DATA

USE
MULTIFAMILY HOUSING
307 RENTAL UNITS

OTHER USE
10,000 SQ FT (930 SQ M) OFFICE

YEAR OPENED
2011

SITE SIZE
3.87 AC (1.56 HA)

RENTAL RATES
$900–$1,600

DEVELOPER/OWNER
AREA REAL ESTATE

ARCHITECT
LAKE/FLATO ARCHITECTS,
O'NEILL CONRAD OPPELT
ARCHITECTS INC. (ARCHITECT OF
RECORD)

LENDER
HUD 221(D)(4) LOAN SECURED
THROUGH ROCKHALL FUNDING

THE 1221 BROADWAY PROJECT WAS THE FIRST major residential development in the long-neglected, formerly industrial neighborhood of River North. The project's proximity to the two-mile (3.2 km) extension of the Riverwalk and the city's commitment to revitalizing this ragged edge of downtown were key reasons AREA Real Estate purchased the abandoned project. Developer David Adelman recognized that the Riverwalk would be a major draw for the project's primary target market—young professionals and empty nesters. "Our residents are renters by choice who are seeking a healthy lifestyle," he says.

Exterior of 1221 Broadway. Fitness classes are held in the open-air parking structure, on the right. *Frank Ooms*

Located 1.5 miles (2.4 km) north of downtown, 1221 Broadway is an adaptive use of a housing development that initially failed during construction in 2007. Occupying three blocks, 1221 Broadway transformed the abandoned concrete super-structure into a four-story structure offering 307 apartments and 10,000 square feet (930 sq m) of ground-floor office space.

Main Wellness Features

FITNESS AMENITIES

Property manager Christian Vargas notes that many residents say they moved to 1221 to be near the Riverwalk, which they can use to walk to restaurants and entertainment and to jog and bike without needing to drive to a gym; the project's Walk Score of 71 confirms that it is in a "very walk-able" location.

On-site elements that encourage exercise and physical fitness include the following:

✳ **Fitness centers.** The developer turned a rarely used space on the fifth floor of a garage into an open-air workout space where classes in high-intensity interval training are held twice a week. Covered with a metal roof, the space is

open to the elements and provides a 360-degree view of the city. The developer subsidizes the classes so residents pay only $5 per class; other, unsubsidized classes were offered but were subsequently canceled because of poor turnout.

Courtyards are the site of many programmed events.
Chris Cooper

Oversized floor-to-ceiling windows bring additional daylight into the residences and offer views of downtown.
Chris Cooper

Yoga classes will be added soon with a similar subsidized agreement with the instructor.

The project features two additional work-out areas: one is a free-weight gym with heavy dumbbells and studio flooring for classes; the other, a gym located next to the heated pool, has cardio equipment and light weights.

✳ **Pools.** Residents can choose between two pools—the rooftop lap pool, heated during the cool season to promote year-round use, and a resort-style pool on the first floor. The cost for heating the rooftop pool is minimal.

✳ **Biking.** In 2013, the developer installed a multitool bike repair station that is available 24 hours a day. The station is regularly used and well worth the minimal cost of only $1,000, says Adelman.

Capitalizing on the proximity of the Riverwalk hiking/biking trail, the developer incorporated a number of other biking amenities, such as the on-site B-Cycle station, which is part of the downtown bike-sharing program, and about 100 outdoor bike racks are available to residents for bike storage.

COURTYARDS AND OUTDOOR STAIRCASES/ SOCIAL INTERACTION

Most of the residences are organized around court-yards, each with a distinct character, which gives a more human scale to the concrete superstructure and creates a collegial feeling, says project architect David Lake. One courtyard has a 12-foot-long (19.3 m) table where residents often eat dinner; another has a barbecue area.

The courtyards are used for programmed events—outdoor movie nights, fitness classes, and food truck dinners several nights a week. Instead of being embedded within the building, the stairs are placed on the outside walls facing the courtyards, thus becoming places where residents can meet their neighbors, Lake says.

The courtyards also bring more light and fresh air into the apartments. Planted with an abundance of trees, the courtyards are shady in the summer and help minimize urban heat-island effects.

The project is unusually welcoming to pets. More than 100 dogs live in the complex. The dog park on the north end of the site is a favorite amenity and gathering place for residents. Annual costs for maintaining the park total about $1,500.

Before and after images show the transformation of 1221 Broadway from an abandoned concrete shell to a residential and office project with pools, fitness classes, and bike amenities.
Chris Cooper (top)
Lake Flato (bottom)

ROY SMITH St.

11 11

AVE A

512 Car Garage

Apt. Over
Retail / Office
Phase 2

4

2

6

9

10

5

BROADWAY

7 8

3

12th St.

0 10 25   50

AVE B

10 10

San Antonio River

Riverwalk North

1. Bridge 2. Pool Court 3. Cypress Court 4. Stair Court 5. The Lawn 6. Blue Court 7. Skyline Pool 8. Pool Room 9. Fitness Center 10. Rainwater Cisterns 11. Existing Houses

ACCESS TO DAYLIGHT

An important selling feature of the apartments is the oversized floor-to-ceiling windows, which bring additional daylight into the residences, offer dramatic views of downtown, and make the units feel larger. "Our apartments have far more day-lighting than any others in the area, which helped distinguish us from our competitors and boosted lease-up," Adelman says. Enlarging the windows on a concrete frame structure was a challenge and costly, but well worth the effort, he says.

Performance

In 2011, the project leased up its first phase of 268 units quickly, achieving 99 percent occupancy within four months. "This was one of the fastest lease-ups in the city," notes Lake, and proved the depth of the market in the River North district. It also proved that residents were willing to pay premium rents for smaller units. The average unit size unit at 1221 Broadway, 725 square feet (67.5 sq m), is about 200 square feet (19 sq m) smaller than typical apartments in the San Antonio area. Rents

exceed pro forma projections, and the developer's rate of return for this first phase was 8.4 percent.

This early success encouraged the developer to build a second phase—an additional 39 apartments above a 10,000-square-foot (930 sq m) single-story building (part of the original structure), which hous-es the developer's and leasing offices, as well as a landscape architecture firm. The development team originally planned a retail/restaurant/entertainment development for this space, but came to recognize that because "we were the first one on the block in this still-evolving neighborhood, there wasn't suffi-cient density to support the retail," says Lake.

The developer secured a HUD 221(d)(4) loan aimed at promoting market-rate projects in blighted areas. "This neighborhood looked like Beirut after the war, and it was difficult to convince private lenders to fund a project here," notes Adelman. The 1221 Broadway project was the catalyst for addition-al development in the previously derelict district—all of which has been funded with private capital, he notes. Multiple commercial projects are underway in the area: more than 800 residential units have been built and about 600 or so are under construction.

1221 Broadway's health and wellness features and amenities are distributed throughout the complex.
Lake Flato

Jackson Walk

Jackson, Tennessee

HEALTHY COMMUNITY LLC WAS SELECTED by the city of Jackson's Community Development Agency to revitalize a 17-acre (7 ha) downtown site, which had been sorely neglected for many years. At about the same time, the city was launching a community-wide health and wellness initiative to make Jackson the healthiest city in the state.

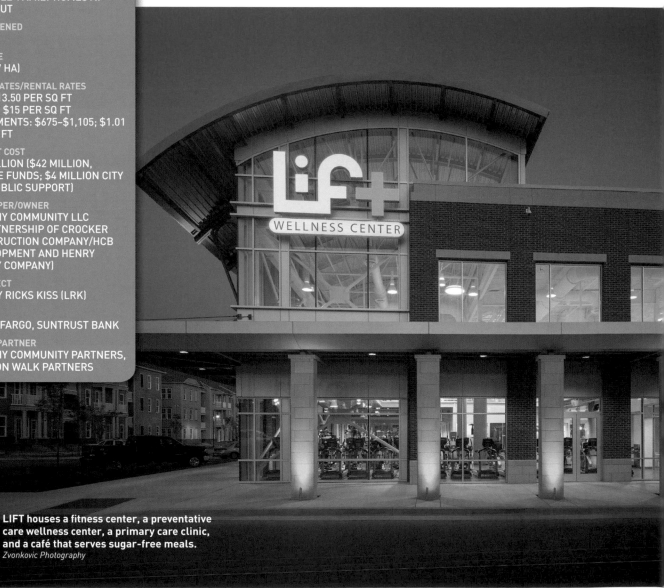

LIFT houses a fitness center, a preventative care wellness center, a primary care clinic, and a café that serves sugar-free meals.
Zvonkovic Photography

In 2010, Tennessee had the second-highest obesity rates in the nation. News that potentially high employee health care costs had discouraged a company from moving to Jackson was the wakeup call, leading to the Jumpstart Jackson initiative, which was intended to boost economic development as well as improve the health of Jackson citizens. Using health and wellness as the redevelopment theme for Jackson Walk, the Healthy Community master developer selected an 82,000-square-foot (7,600 sq m) medical care–based LIFT (Living in a Fit Tennessee) fitness/wellness center as the site's main anchor, creating a new type of anchor for the downtown as well.

"Caring for your city is analogous to taking charge of your health," says Hal Crocker, president of HCB Development, one of two partners that formed Healthy Community LLC. "Restoring an ailing part of downtown is vital to a city's health and long-term prosperity, much the way caring for yourself contributes to better health and a longer life."

This infill redevelopment features the combination fitness center/wellness center and primary care clinic, some retail space, and apartments. In addition, new single-family homes, a city-owned amphitheater, and a dog park create a new neighborhood around this center.

Main Wellness Features

FITNESS CENTER/WELLNESS CENTER/CLINIC AS AN ANCHOR

LIFT, which is operated by West Tennessee Healthcare, is the Jackson area's only medical fitness center and had first considered a suburban location before deciding to partner with Healthy Community. The LIFT building houses a fitness center, a preventative care wellness center, a primary care clinic, and a café that serves sugar-free meals for diabetics and calorie-conscious diners. The largest element, the fitness center, includes a gym with a basketball court, indoor pools, cardiovascular and strength-training equipment, and an indoor walking track.

The wellness center offers physical and occupational therapy; cardio and orthopedic rehab; and programs focused on women's health. The center holds numerous outreach events at schools and seniors' centers, and has an extensive disease-management program that offers free educational programs on diabetes and congestive heart failure. The center's corporate-wellness program partners with Jackson businesses to offer preventative care resources and guidance to employees. The developer worked closely with the three main employers downtown—city hall, the county courthouse, and the Jackson Energy Authority—which all purchased fitness center memberships for their employees.

LIFT has become the hub for health activities in Jackson and sponsors numerous community events, including monthly five-kilometer runs, obstacle course runs, and high-speed bicycle races that attract several thousand people. Many groups use Jackson Walk's walking trails as part of their event route.

The developer notes that the fitness center and rehab components work well together. For example, after completing their rehab program, individuals have the option to continue pursuing long-term fitness goals and join the fitness center. Because the LIFT center is a medical care–based

LIFT Wellness Center serves as an anchor for the newly redeveloped site and a fitness hub for the city of Jackson. *Looney Ricks Kiss*

fitness facility, its members tend to be older than those at a typical gym; many are retired. As a result, the facility is busy throughout the day rather than attracting peak use before and after work, which benefits the development's 20,000-square-foot (1,900 sq m) retail component.

Healthy Community's retail strategy is to target retailers providing synergy with the health-related theme and the pedestrian-oriented community. Of the total $44 million in development costs, $17 million was spent on the LIFT facility.

DESIGN FOR PEDESTRIANS AND BICYCLISTS

The developers recognized the importance of making healthy choices convenient. The ability to reach three of the city's largest employers as well

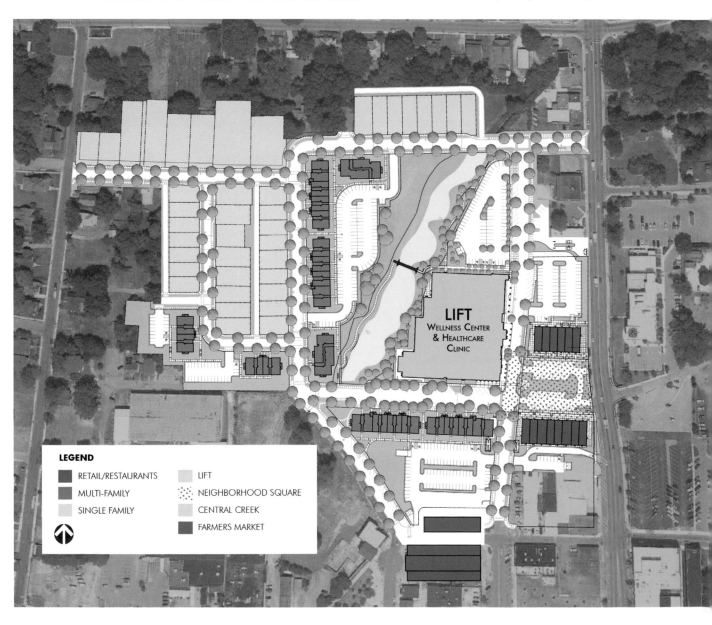

LEGEND

- RETAIL/RESTAURANTS
- MULTI-FAMILY
- SINGLE FAMILY
- LIFT
- NEIGHBORHOOD SQUARE
- CENTRAL CREEK
- FARMERS MARKET

as the West Tennessee Farmers' Market on foot or by bike was a key factor in the developer's decision to redevelop the site. The University of Memphis Lambuth Campus is also a walk or bicycle ride away. In addition, Jackson Walk residents have easy access to the amenities and services provided in the multiuse neighborhood. The site has a Walk Score of 72, indicating it is "very walkable."

On-site strategies include a parklike setting, with an unsightly concrete drainage artery transformed into an attractive water feature, and a 1.5-mile (2.4 km) walking trail with exercise stations. Additional walking and biking paths connect the site with downtown and midtown neighborhoods.

To balance the convenience required by a medical facility with the parklike ambience, automobile parking was split into smaller segments rather than provided in one large lot; some parking was tucked behind the commercial buildings. The developer undertook parking studies, which identified opportunities for shared parking and helped convince potential retail tenants and the operators of LIFT that it was not necessary to surround the commercial development with a sea of parking.

Performance

The LIFT facility, which opened in January 2013 and has attracted more 3,000 members, exceeded membership and financial projections in its first year. The developer attributes much of LIFT's success to the pedestrian-friendly setting, with shopping and restaurants nearby. Center members can walk or drive to the gym, then visit the nearby dry cleaner, grab a quick lunch, or visit the farmers' market without having to drive to each destination.

Sixty percent of members live within eight miles (13 km) of the center, and the remaining members come from throughout the region, bringing new life to the area.

The upscale apartments attract young, mostly single professionals who like the ambience of downtown living, and older empty nesters, who like living in a neighborhood where many amenities are within easy walking distance, including the farmers market, downtown businesses and the entertainment district, the new city-owned outdoor amphitheater (opened spring 2014), and the dog park.

At buildout, Jackson Walk will also have 32 new single-family homes, including 12 smaller homes—1,300 to 1,650 square feet (120 to 150 sq m)—that will be offered through special grant

incentives from the city for first-time homebuyers, and 20 larger homes at 2,400 square feet (220 sq m). So far, Crocker has built four smaller homes: two have sold, for $115,000 and $122,000. A model home for the larger-style residences, which opened five months ago, is priced at $209,000. "Considering that these were the first homes built in this part of the city in more than 40 years, it's early, and we're still overcoming perception issues typical of revitalization projects. But we are well ahead of where we expected to be at this time," says Crocker.

The decision to make health and wellness the dominant theme at Jackson Walk was "not just the morally right thing to do, it made economic sense," says codeveloper Henry Turley.

Meanwhile, the city's Jumpstart Jackson initiative, which encourages citizens to "eat right, get out, and get active," is credited with helping reduce city employee health care costs. And Jackson's community-wide health and wellness initiative prompted the U.S. Conference of Mayors to select Jackson in 2013 as one of the most livable cities in America in the small cities category.

The West Tennessee Farmers' Market, providing city residents with access to fresh and local food, is located at the southern edge of the site.
Nona Brummett

The Century Building
Pittsburgh, Pennsylvania

PROJECT DATA

USE
MIXED USE
60 WORKFORCE AND MARKET-
RATE APARTMENTS
12,000 SQ FT (1,100 SQ M) OFFICE
10,000 SQ FT (900 SQ M) RETAIL

YEAR OPENED
2009

SITE SIZE
8,000 SQ FT (743 SQ M)

RENTAL RATES/LEASE RATES
MARKET-RATE APARTMENTS:
$1,050–$1,550 FOR 1–2
BEDROOMS

OFFICE: AVERAGE $18 PER SQ FT

RETAIL: OVER $20 PER SQ FT

PROJECT COST
$18 MILLION

DEVELOPER/OWNER
TREK DEVELOPMENT GROUP

ARCHITECT
KONING EIZENBERG ARCHITECTS,
MOSHIER STUDIOS

FINANCING
SEVEN PUBLIC, PRIVATE, AND
NONPROFIT FUNDING SOURCES

SINCE THE LATE 1990S, DOWNTOWN PITTSBURGH has been experiencing a housing renaissance, largely for higher-income households. The redeveloped Century Building, which opened in 2009 with 28 affordable workforce units and 32 market-rate housing units, was the first affordable housing built downtown. Working with the Pittsburgh Downtown Partnership and other civic groups on their goal of encouraging provision of workforce housing in central Pittsburgh, developer TREK Development Group had both a personal commitment

The redeveloped Century Building provided the first workforce housing units in downtown Pittsburgh.
Eric Staudenmaier Photography

and business motivation for achieving high standards for sustainability. "The market is increasingly demanding sustainable features, including ones that promote an active, healthy lifestyle," observes William Gatti, president of TREK.

The 12-story, 80,000-square-foot (7,400 sq m), formerly underused 1907 office building in the downtown cultural district was redeveloped to provide housing for 60 residents, as well as two floors of office space and a restaurant. It was the first residential development in the city to achieve LEED Gold certification and has a Walk Score of 100, indicating the location is a "walker's paradise."

Main Wellness Features

About 15 percent of the construction budget was devoted to green and wellness features.

CLEAN INDOOR AIR

Residents routinely inform the building management that their asthma and allergies have improved since they moved to the building. Strategies for clean indoor air include the following:

* A nonsmoking policy, unusual for the market, which helped the project achieve LEED Gold. About six residents have been reprimanded for smoking, but only one resident has had to leave because of the policy.
* Use of low-VOC paints and nontoxic materials throughout the residences.
* A consistent level of heating and cooling provided by the building's open-loop, electric geothermal system. The system, which cost 5 percent more than a conventional HVAC system, operates at roughly 30 percent savings compared with conventional systems. In severely cold weather, a backup gas boiler and cooling tower are used to supplement the geothermal system.

TREK had used geothermal systems in its projects regularly in the past ten years. Because these open-loop systems draw water from an aquifer, Gatti says it is important to pay attention to water quality, which can change over time. For example, the iron content may increase, which can create problems for the heat exchanger. "It's important that your maintenance person has the requisite skills to

A nonsmoking policy and the use of nontoxic building materials have a positive impact on residents' allergies and asthma.
Eric Staudenmaier Photography

care for these more complicated, specialized systems."

＊ An energy-recovery wheel, used to heat the common spaces, which creates positive pressure in the hallways, effectively removing the smell of spillover cooking odors from the building. The recovery ventilation system also provides fresh air when windows are closed.

BICYCLE COMMUTER CENTER

"We wanted to promote bicycle usage in a meaningful and elegant way," notes Gatti, whose firm teamed with the Pittsburgh Cultural Trust, Pittsburgh Downtown Partnership, and Southwestern Pennsylvania Commission to create an on-site bicycle commuter center. Largely funded by a grant from the Federal Transit Administration, the center provides secure bike storage for residents and is available to the office tenants and other city commuters for $125 a year; about half the 49 spaces

The prominent bicycle commuter center promotes bicycle use for residents and other city bikers.
Eric Staudenmaier Photography

are used by residents. Constructed of recycled shipping containers, the green-painted center was inexpensive to construct, and maintenance fees are minimal—about $1,000 a year, including utilities. The primary cost is lighting the structure and hosing it down once a year. On the first three stories of the north building wall behind the center, the developer painted a bright green billboard with a bicycle graphic as a way to call attention to the center and welcome the biking community.

FITNESS CENTER

The building's fitness room has eight pieces of equipment and a dumbbell rack. It cost about $25,000 to equip the room; maintenance costs are minimal.

Performance

When the renovation was completed in August 2009, the Century Building was fully leased within 90 days—six months ahead of schedule. Over the years, TREK has raised the rents for all the housing units, which are exceeding pro-forma projections. According to Gatti, the location, the product, and the price all helped make the development successful, but it is the green and wellness features that are the main attraction. "Anyone in the industry who is not intently focused on sustainability and health is behind the curve," he notes. "This is what the consumer expects." Moreover, these are the features that have contributed to the building's remarkably high 90 percent retention rate, he says.

Via6
Ben Benschneider

Via6
Seattle, Washington

PROJECT DATA

USE
MULTIFAMILY HOUSING
654 STUDIO, ONE-, AND TWO-
BEDROOM UNITS

YEAR OPENED
2013

SITE SIZE
0.89 AC (0.36 HA)

RENTAL RATES
$1,400 TO $4,380

PROJECT COST
$193 MILLION

DEVELOPER
PINE STREET GROUP LLC

ARCHITECT/INTERIOR DESIGNER
GGLO

EQUITY PARTNERS
CANADA PENSION PLAN
INVESTMENT BOARD AND THE
MULTI-EMPLOYER PROPERTY
TRUST, CLIENTS OF BENTALL
KENNEDY, SEATTLE.

BEFORE THE PINE STREET GROUP CONCEIVED OF VIA6, its adjacent blocks had no housing, very little street life, and few amenities. The design for Via6 was started with the objective of building a community rather than building an apartment building, says Matt Griffin, principal and managing partner of Pine Street Group. Taking that approach changed the way his company thought about designing and marketing the project. Via6 is not only the first apartment building Pine Street Group has developed, but also the largest residential project in downtown Seattle built in one phase.

The design for Via6 was started with the objective of building a community rather than building an apartment building.
Tim Rice Architectural Photography

Griffin was inspired to create a place where people wanted to stay, as well as where they could live without needing to own a car. Via6 is located two blocks from the Westlake Transit Hub, which connects people to all reaches of the city.

Via6 is a 24-story, two-tower mixed-use project spanning the length of one downtown block. It has 654 studio and one- and two-bedroom apartments located above 15,000 square feet (1,400 sq m) of community-oriented service businesses.

Main Wellness Features

Location aside, by focusing on building a community rather than an apartment building, Pine Street Group created a project that includes features that strongly promote both physical activity and social interaction—features that can be adapted in other projects. Establishing this sense of community is a big part of what sets Via6 apart from similar apartment complexes.

With a perfect Walk Score of 100, the site is ideal for promoting walkability and bikability— and removing the need for car ownership. Griffin believes that a car-free lifestyle is a way to reduce the stress (as well as the cost) that comes with car ownership. Though the units are smaller than most in the Seattle area—averaging 715 square feet (66 sq m)—Griffin noted "the location is so good that over time we believe people will pay a premium to be here."

SPACES FOR COMMUNITY GATHERING AND SOCIAL CONNECTIONS

Creating spaces and opportunities for planned and spontaneous social interaction was a major factor in the design and remains a focus of operations of Via6. The original motivation for creating this sense of community was to retain tenants, Griffin says, but he now believes that if people know their neighbors, they will be healthier as well. Community-supporting wellness features include:

* **Ground-floor public uses.** A restaurant, grocery store, coffee shop, barber shop, and bike shop are used by both residents and the general public, providing both convenience to residents and chances to meet others in the neighborhood.
* **An 18-foot (5.5 m) steel-clad chronograph located in the lobby.** Residents and guests can click through topics displayed on the chronograph to see what is trending online and get the latest headlines. The chronograph also displays

The seventh-floor pavilion includes indoor and outdoor spaces that encourage resident interaction.
Ben Benschneider

An 18-foot (5.5 m) chronograph in the lobby displays information about Via6 and the neighborhood.
Ben Benschneider

A mezzanine level contains social amenities and games for residents and is visible from the lobby below.
Ben Benschneider

information about Via6, and neighborhood amenities and services—all of which provide people with information that will help them strike up conversations with one another.

✳ **A mezzanine level where activity is visible from the lobby.** Amenities located there include

pool tables and shuffleboard tables, and easy chairs with tables. Abundant power outlets and free wifi encourage residents to come down from their units to work or relax during evenings and weekends, allowing people to meet

Bicycle amenities feature prominently within the ground and mezzanine levels of Via6.
Pine Street Group

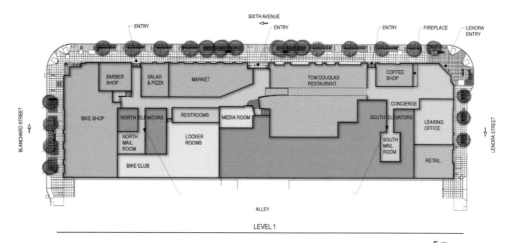

LEVEL 1

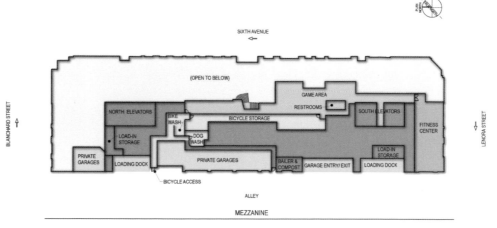

MEZZANINE

without having to go down to the street-level bars and restaurants.

* **A ground-floor theater area.** The theater can be reserved for private events but is open to all residents when local sports teams are playing. Residents who are sports fans can watch their favorite teams in a social setting with other fans rather than watching in their own apartment.

* **The pavilion.** An area on the seventh floor between the two towers, referred to as the pavilion, has indoor and outdoor space that can be used nearly year-round due to Seattle's temperate climate. Instead of individual grills, the area has three large barbecues with multiple controls, as well as communal tables, encouraging residents to cook and eat alongside their neighbors. Griffin says he has been amazed by the number of people who first met in this space.

* **In-house event coordinators.** During the first year, a husband-and-wife musician/artist team has lived at Via6 rent-free in exchange for planning social events for residents to meet their neighbors.

SUPPORT AND AMENITIES FOR BIKING

Via6 has embraced the notion of bikability not only for residents, but also for the broader downtown community. Griffin convinced the popular Velo Bike Shop—located in another neighborhood for 24 years—to relocate to Via6 to help with this vision.

Pine Street Group also built space for ViaBike, a bike club for downtown bicycle commuters that is managed by Velo. For a monthly fee of $15, the club provides secure storage for 150 bikes, private access to the club off an alley, and locker rooms with showers and towel service. Members' bikes parked in designated stalls can be serviced by Velo while their owners are at work.

Bike storage for residents is separate and is reached by a ramp off the alley. Residents also have access to a bike wash, air pump, and stands

with bike tools. The bike shop offers classes for residents on changing flat tires and performing other minor maintenance. The shop also reserves a few bikes for lending to residents at no cost for running errands. These features, which have made Via6 known as a hub for bicyclists, have played a big role in marketing the building to prospective residents and retail tenants, and in creating a health-focused identity for the project, says Griffin.

Performance

Via6 has performed better than expected in terms of income, Griffin says, though the Pine Street Group measures early success more by lease-up rate than lease premiums. The firm expected it would take 18 months for the project to be 90 percent leased, but it took less than a year, despite the small unit size and an increased apartment supply in Seattle. Rents range from $1,175 to $4,285 per month, and Griffin notes that Via6 is pushing rent rates higher in Seattle. Rents at Via6 currently average about $3 per square foot.

Left: ViaBike, a bike club for downtown bicycle commuters, provides secure bike storage for club members. Bike storage for Via6 residents is separate.
Ben Benschneider

Right: The Velo Bike Shop, which relocated to Via6, serves as a bicycling hub for the whole neighborhood.
Ben Benschneider

The Interlace
Singapore

PROJECT DATA

USE
MULTIFAMILY RESIDENTIAL
1,040 CONDOMINIUM UNITS

OTHER USE
500 SQ M (5,400 SQ FT) RETAIL

YEAR OPENED
2013

SITE SIZE
8 HA (19.8 AC)

SALES PRICES
S$9,150–S$11,300 PER SQ M

PROJECT COST
S$1.44 BILLION (US$1.14 BILLION)
(APPROX.)

DEVELOPER
CAPITALAND SINGAPORE LIMITED

DESIGNER
OFFICE FOR METROPOLITAN
ARCHITECTURE (OMA)

ARCHITECT
RSP ARCHITECTS PLANNERS &
ENGINEERS (PTE.) LTD.

EQUITY PARTNERS
HOTEL PROPERTIES LTD. AND
ONE OTHER SHAREHOLDER

THE INTERLACE IS ONE OF THE LARGEST RESIDENTIAL DEVELOPMENTS in Singapore. The 24-story complex in Singapore's District 4 has 1,040 residential condo units, ranging from two to four bedrooms to penthouse units, as well as eight retail shops. Seeking a solution in the face of scarce open space and controls on floor/area ratios, the architect for the Interlace was "inspired by the old villages of Singapore," says Ong Sim Lian, senior vice president for design management at developer CapitaLand Singapore Limited (CLS).

Multiple fitness amenities aimed at promoting a healthy lifestyle were incorporated, including a 50-meter (164 ft) lap pool.
CapitaLand Singapore/ Woh Hup (Private) Limited

Designed by Ole Scheeren, who was then the partner in the Office for Metropolitan Architecture (OMA), the Interlace breaks away from the standard typology of residential developments in Singapore, which typically are composed of a cluster of isolated, vertical towers. At the Interlace, 31 apartment blocks, each six stories tall, are stacked in a hexagonal arrangement to form eight large-scale courtyards. The interlocking blocks resemble a "vertical village" with cascading rooftop gardens and terraces. "This arrangement allows for porosity of views, ventilation, and green spaces to be spread throughout all levels," says Ong.

During the concept and design phase, wind and sun test analyses were conducted to maximize the benefit of shade in Singapore's tropical climate. These tests helped determine the placement of facilities and bodies of water to allow passive cooling of the environment, thus encouraging outdoor activities.

Main Wellness Features

DESIGN FOR PHYSICAL ACTIVITY

The Interlace provides a wide range of facilities promoting a healthy lifestyle. The developer estimates that expenses for the outdoor amenities account for about 50 percent of the project's operating budget. The project's physical-fitness facilities include the following:

* **A one-kilometer (0.6 mi) jogging track around the perimeter of the main complex.** Because the project is large, CLS has been able to build this feature into the design since its conception. The track, four meters (13 ft) wide, doubles as access for fire and emergency response vehicles, which have the same width.
* **A 50-meter (164 ft) Olympic-sized lap pool** "to encourage 'serious' swimming," says Ong, as well as a series of play pools. The lap pool is a main feature provided in most of CapitaLand's developments.

A one-kilometer (0.6 mi) jogging track surrounds the complex.
CapitaLand Singapore

* **A cluster of three tennis courts and one multi-purpose court,** positioned along one side of the blocks.
* **A 280-square-meter (3,000 sq ft) gym** with 26 pieces of equipment.

OUTDOOR AMENITIES/SOCIAL INTERACTION

The developer considers ample open space a vital feature of the project. Parking and bike storage are located underground, freeing up space at ground level and above. Creating vast green spaces by extending the landscape vertically, the Interlace's ground landscape spans 66,641 square meters (717,300 sq ft). CapitaLand notes that all these open spaces combined amount to over 112 percent of the original land area. By maximizing green coverage, the Interlace ultimately extends living spaces outdoors for all its residents.

The primary outdoor spaces are:
* Eight hexagonal courtyards, each with a different theme and measuring 56 meters (184 ft) in diameter. The developer noted that the variation in theme for the outdoor spaces is important to encourage community bonding and social gatherings to take place. One courtyard has a community garden that will be used by the residents' garden club; another courtyard caters to children and includes a family-friendly playground. Other courtyards have pavilions, spa pools with Jacuzzis and rainshowers, barbecue pits, a dog run area, and outdoor fitness equipment.
* Nine "sky garden" roof terraces accessible to all residents. These sky gardens together with private roof terraces cover a total area of 23,588 square meters (253,889 sq ft).

AGING-IN-PLACE UNITS

The Interlace has features that appeal to multi-generational families. One-eighth of the units are aging-in-place (AIP) units with provisions that cater to senior residents—for instance, bathroom access. In Singapore, bathrooms are traditionally separated

The Interlace is made up of 31 stacked blocks forming eight courtyard areas. The interlocking blocks allow for views, ventilation, and green spaces at all levels. *CapitaLand Singapore*

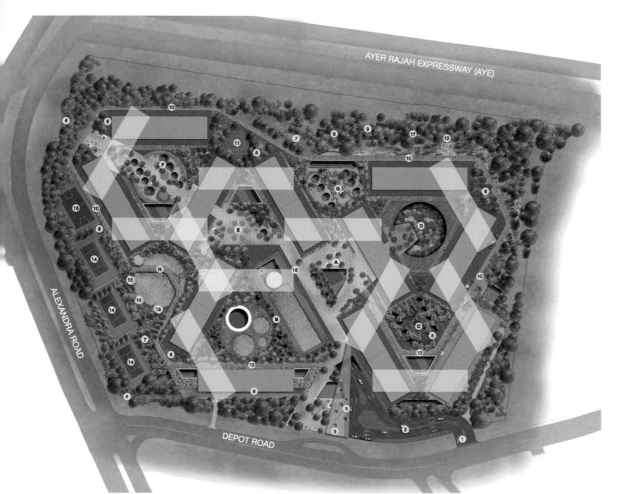

LANDSCAPE COURTYARDS

A.	Central Square
B.	Water Park
C.	Play Hills
D.	Spa Valley
E.	Theatre Plaza
F.	Bamboo Garden
G.	Lotus Pond
H.	Waterfall Terrace

FACILITIES

1. Main Entrance
2. Guard House
3. Pedestrian Main Gate
4. Pedestrian Side Gate
5. Drop-off
6. Retail Plaza
7. Play Zone
8. Outdoor Exercise Station
9. BBQ Promenade
10. Jogging Track
11. Gardening Zone
12. Pet Zone
13. Party Pavillion
14. Tennis Court
15. Multi-purpose Court
16. Clubhouse (1st Storey)
17. Putting Green

from other rooms with a drop of about 2.5 to 5 centimeters (1 to 2 in). In the Interlace's AIP units, those drops have been removed, making the units wheelchair-friendly.

The public spaces in the Interlace follow universal design principles, allowing residents of any age to gain access to them and enjoy the project's amenities. For instance, the state-of-the-art fitness center includes wheelchair-accessible weight machines. For incorporating multiple universal design features, the Interlace has been awarded the Gold Plus (Design) by Singapore's Building Construction Authority.

Performance

More than 80 percent of these units were sold before the developer obtained a temporary occupation permit (TOP) in September 2013; the TOP is granted when basic building requirements and amenities such as water and sanitary components have been approved by authorities. According to the developer, there has been a 10 percent increase in the sales premiums since the launch.

Themed courtyards such as a community garden (pictured) and kids' playground promote social interaction between residents.
CapitaLand Singapore

Park 20|20
Haarlemmermeer, Netherlands

DELTA DEVELOPMENT GROUP, DEVELOPER OF PARK 20|20, was inspired to follow the Cradle-to-Cradle (C2C) philosophy, a development strategy conceived by architect William McDonough, the master planner for the project, and chemist Michael Braungart. The C2C platform is "a human-centered design," notes Owen Zachariasse, innovations and sustainability manager for Delta, "meaning building occupants are central to all design choices we make."

PROJECT DATA

USE
OFFICE
160,000 SQ FT (14,900 SQ M)
OFFICE, PHASE I
127,350 SQ FT (11,831 SQ M)
OFFICE, PHASE IIA
RETAIL AND HOTEL AT BUILDOUT

YEAR OPENED
2013

SITE SIZE
11 HA (28 AC)

LEASE RATES
€200 PER SQ M OFFICE

PROJECT COST
€65.4 MILLION (US$89.5 MILLION)
FOR PHASE I

DEVELOPER/OWNER
DELTA DEVELOPMENT GROUP

ARCHITECT
WILLIAM McDONOUGH +
PARTNERS

FINANCING
REGGEBORGH GROEP

ENGINEER
ROYAL VOLKERWESSELS STEIN
N.V.

A spine of greenhouses spans the park in the center of the development.
Delta Development Group

Park 20|20 is an 11-hectare (28 ac) mixed-use business park about eight kilometers (5 mi) southwest of Amsterdam. The first phase of the project was delivered in April 2013, and additional stages are to be completed by 2018.

Main Wellness Features

The site sits only 100 meters (330 feet) from train and bus transit and has a Walk Score of 72, which indicates a "very walkable" location.

On site and within the context of its overarching C2C strategy focusing on building high-quality and sustainable spaces, Delta has provided the following wellness components for Park 20|20.

CLEAN INDOOR AIR

A Slimline floor system with a 70-millimeter-thick (2.8 in) concrete core was implemented in buildings to allow for air circulation, heating, and cooling. This concrete-and-steel subfloor allows for radiant heating, eliminating the need for much of the traditional ductwork that requires regular cleaning and can blow dust particles into the office space. All office buildings in Park 20|20 contain operable windows

as well, allowing fresh air to enter directly from outside.

The developer also incorporated green walls as secondary air filtration techniques. Interior green features were employed to sequester carbon dioxide and produce oxygen. Plants for the green walls in building atriums were selected according to their ability to live indoors with little water and light, and the amount of oxygen they produce. Moss was used to back partitions separating work areas as a sound buffer and as a natural dust filter.

NATURAL AND LED LIGHTING

Though the Netherlands has an office lighting code requiring 500 lux of artificial light per workspace, Delta exceeded those by also providing natural lighting at minimal cost at Park 20|20. Buildings are designed in a horseshoe shape, with large atriums allowing light to permeate indoor spaces from two sides.

For artificial lighting, the developer employed LED lights as much as possible—the closest lighting type to sunlight—with a combination of general and task lighting. Traditional halogen lights give off too much heat and can lead to worker fatigue,

Walking and biking paths traverse the site's nine hectares (22 ac) of open space.
Delta Development Group

says Zachariasse. Even so, the natural lighting at Park 20|20 is so effective that Zachariasse notes he has "not once seen the task lighting turned on." In addition, Park 20|20 buildings use an automated MechoShade sun-shading system to regulate lighting—the first project in the Netherlands to do so. The system reads cloud cover and automatically adjusts interior lights to create the best possible environment for occupants.

To address the higher investment costs of LED lighting compared with traditional halogen lights, Delta is renting the lighting system from lighting supplier LED Lease. Each year, Delta calculates the amount it expects to spend for lighting and pays that amount upfront to LED Lease. At year's end, Delta compares that amount with the actual energy consumed and settles the difference, getting a rebate if its electricity use is lower than projected. Renting the LED system—or "leasing light"—is cost-effective: "Both Park 20|20 and our company have the [financial] incentive to save energy to the greatest extent possible," says Gijs de Rooij, CEO of LED Lease. This process eliminates the initial investment for purchasing the higher-cost LED system, and Delta has received rebates on the estimated rental expense.

Park 20|20 is a car-free site at ground level.
William McDonough + Partners

DESIGN FOR PEDESTRIANS AND FITNESS

Park 20|20 is a car-free site at ground level. Multiple walking and biking paths traverse the site, connecting nine hectares (22 ac) of open space, including an entire park and buildings that sit above parking. One notable aspect of the site design is the central park's visibility from surrounding streets, creating a more open and inviting space. Parking is provided in underground garages reached at the perimeter of the property, adjacent to pedestrian access points.

Park 20|20 offers a fitness program that is also available to employers located off site. The developer collaborated with the municipal government, which provides trainers for fitness classes both indoors in the gym and outdoors. Both the upkeep of the gym and the classes are paid for by tenant association dues.

COMMUNITY GARDENS/SOCIAL INTERACTION

Two greenhouses have been completed in the first development phase, part of a spine of greenhouses under construction that will span the middle of the development. The greenhouses are already producing food that is purchased by Delta's on-site

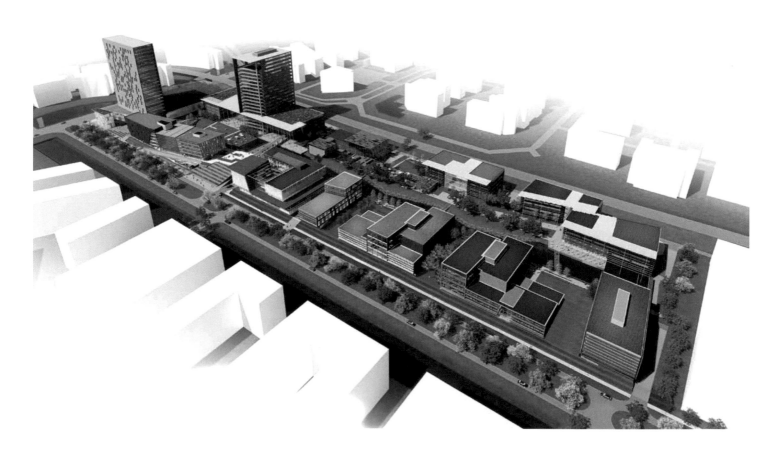

Plants for the green walls in building atriums were selected for the amount of oxygen they produce, as well as their ability to live indoors. *Foppe + Schut*

restaurant; the remaining food is sold to another local restaurant.

The greenhouses are available for use by anyone who works at Park 20|20, as well as provide a work opportunity for local seniors and other city residents. To scale up the garden initiative, Delta Development is looking to provide similar greenhouses at future projects in order to incorporate Park 20|20 into a wider urban farming concept.

CLEAN OUTDOOR AIR

The green roofs installed on all buildings not only provide a safe habitat for migrating birds, but also absorb particles from the outdoor environment. Park 20|20 is near Amsterdam's Schiphol Airport, so outdoor air purification is especially important.

Performance

Park 20|20 is currently 100 percent leased and lease rates are €200 per square meter, a premium of about 12 percent over other local Class A new-build offices. Phase II office buildings, now under construction, are also 100 percent pre-leased.

One major challenge for the developer was expressing its vision to the project's contractors. Delta's philosophy meant that major adjustments had to be made in the development process, particularly in the contractors' approach. "The industry is not adverse to change," says Zachariasse. "It's petrified of change." In order that they might share Delta's perspective and methods, all contractors, architects, and other project partners were trained in C2C design standards and principles by Braungart's consulting company EPEA GmbH.

A key element of Delta's development process was the integration of its supply chain into the design and approval process. Delta first conducted a broad-based study of the availability of C2C-certified materials, offering some distributors preferred materials status, and then informed the general contractor of its findings. This process took place as early as possible in the design process. Although this ran counter to the traditional supply chain approach—which involves "playing a waiting game" in an attempt to acquire materials at the cheapest prices, says Zachariasse—Delta was able to retain the highest value in its final product.

Overall, the cost of materials was not significantly higher than for those used in a more traditional development, Zachariasse says, and Delta may even see savings, especially by buildout of the project's later phases. So far, there has been a reduction in construction costs of 14.8 percent per square meter.

Studies

According to a press release in late 2013 by the Arizona State University Global Sustainability Solutions Center (GSSC) at Haarlemmermeer, GSSC will conduct research and analysis for Park 20|20 in order to assess the links between employee and firm productivity and the built environment.

Via Verde
New York, New York

PROJECT DATA

USE
MIXED-INCOME MULTIFAMILY
71 WORKFORCE CO-OPS,
151 LOW-INCOME RENTAL
APARTMENTS

OTHER USES
5,500 SQ FT (510 SQ M) MEDICAL
CENTER
2,000 SQ FT (185 SQ M) PHARMACY

YEAR OPENED
2012

SITE SIZE
1.5 AC (0.6 HA)

PROJECT COST
$98.8 MILLION

DEVELOPERS/OWNERS
PHIPPS HOUSES, JONATHAN ROSE
COMPANIES

ARCHITECTS
DATTNER ARCHITECTS,
GRIMSHAW ARCHITECTS, LEE
WEINTRAUB LANDSCAPE
ARCHITECTURE

FINANCING
19 PUBLIC, PRIVATE, AND
NONPROFIT FUNDING SOURCES

FOR DETAILS, SEE ULI.ORG/CASE-
STUDY/ULI-CASE-STUDIES-VIA-
VERDE/.

VIA VERDE WAS THE WINNING RESPONSE IN 2006 to the city's first juried design competition for affordable, sustainable housing. In early meetings with the city, South Bronx residents voiced concerns about their unhealthy neighborhood, characterized by a lack of safe places for physical exercise and low-quality housing with high levels of pollutants and noxious chemicals, known contributors to asthma. The South Bronx at the time had among the highest rates of asthma nationwide and high obesity rates. "This feedback from local residents influenced our decision to make health a dominant theme of Via Verde," says Paul Freitag, managing director of project coowner/developer Jonathan Rose Companies.

Via Verde has an abundance of safe spaces for play and physical activity.
Jonathan Rose Companies

Via Verde was codeveloped by Jonathan Rose Companies and Phipps Houses on a city-owned site in the South Bronx, New York, as a public/private partnership. The 6,400-square-foot (595 sq m) mixed-income development—combining high-rise and mid-rise housing, townhouses, and a health clinic and pharmacy—features rental apartments and co-op units. It has a Walk Score of 82, indicating a "very walkable" location.

Although the project cost about 10 percent more than a typical project its size, only a small portion of the excess cost went into green features (the developer estimates about 3 percent). The other cost increases were associated with remediation required by the brownfield site, the expense of high-rise construction, and poor geotechnical conditions.

Main Wellness Features

CLEAN INDOOR AIR

The LEED Gold–certified development uses various strategies to ensure good indoor air quality, among them use of nontoxic low/non-VOC paints, sealants, and adhesives throughout the buildings. Freitag says one great success of LEED is that by calling attention to air quality and health issues, it has led to a larger selection and greater availability of relatively inexpensive non-VOC products and healthy building materials in local stores.

DESIGN FOR PHYSICAL ACTIVITY

* **Active staircases.** Stairways at Via Verde—placed prominently next to entrances to encourage res-

idents to walk instead of using elevators—follow New York City's 2010 Active Design Guidelines, which calls for stairwells that are accessible, visible, and well lit. In contrast to the dark, foreboding cinderblock stairwells of older buildings, Via Verde stairwells have bright paint and wide windows to let in light and make residents feel secure and comfortable. The developer originally planned to provide music in the stairwells, but ran into a snag with city regulations. However, he plans to offer music in the stairwells of a project in Philadelphia.

Stairs at Via Verde also have signs to encourage their use. "People adjust their behavior based on these prompts," says Freitag, "so it's about incentivizing behavior changes and designing a building to reinforce that."

Outdoor stairs connect a series of green roofs, forming a rooftop garden walk to reach

Outdoor stairs connect a series of green roofs and form a rooftop garden walk to reach Via Verde's orchard and gardens. *Jonathan Rose Companies*

Various types of gardens are integrated throughout Via Verde. *Dattner Architects/Grimshaw Architects*

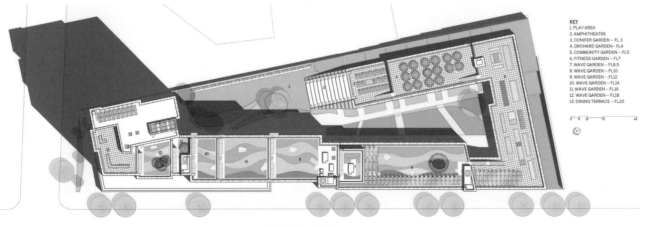

KEY
1. PLAY AREA
2. AMPHITHEATRE
3. CONIFER GARDEN – FL 3
4. ORCHARD GARDEN – FL4
5. COMMUNITY GARDEN – FL5
6. FITNESS GARDEN – FL7
7. WAVE GARDEN – FL8.5
8. WAVE GARDEN – FL10
9. WAVE GARDEN – FL12
10. WAVE GARDEN – FL14
11. WAVE GARDEN – FL16
12. WAVE GARDEN – FL18
13. DINING TERRACE – FL20

BROOK AVE

BERGEN AVE

Vegetable gardens and orchards provide residents with fresh produce and opportunities to learn about gardening.
Jonathan Rose Companies

The interiors of the units feature nontoxic and low-VOC materials to provide clean indoor air.
Jonathan Rose Companies

the apple orchard and vegetable gardens on the fourth and fifth floors. (The name Via Verde means "green way" in Spanish). Next to the fitness center on the seventh floor, the landscaped area used for outdoor exercise classes and social events completes the promenade. "We designed the stairs as an architectural feature and made the walk interesting and beautiful so that by the time people reach the green roof on the seventh floor, they don't realize that they have climbed seven stories," says Freitag. Although walking the stairs is encouraged, all parts of the development, including the garden roofs, are handicapped accessible.

* **Bike storage.** Freitag notes that bike rooms have evolved into a desirable building amenity. The main

cost associated with the bike storage room was the loss of leasable space given over to the room.

* **Fitness center.** Opportunities for exercise and activity are provided at the fitness center, where residents can exercise or take yoga and cardio classes; Pilates classes for children are planned. Partnerships with various nonprofits, including Montefiore Hospital, allow the developer to offer these classes for free.

* **Urban agriculture/social interaction.** The dominant image of Via Verde is the series of terraced green roofs that cascade from the top of the 20-story high-rise to the rooftops of the lower-elevation buildings, then to a ground-level courtyard with an amphitheater. "Green roofs provide many benefits, including dissipating

heat-island effect, building insulation, and absorbing rainwater," Freitag notes. "Also, we wanted them to function as a building amenity that residents could enjoy. So we decided to create opportunities for urban agriculture, where residents could grow fresh produce, socialize with their neighbors, or just relax." Moreover, the South Bronx was a food desert, a problem the roof orchards and vegetable gardens at Via Verde address.

The developer contracted with GrowNYC, a nonprofit that sets up urban gardens throughout the city, to plant the gardens at Via Verde. The first growing season produced an impressive harvest of 1,000 pounds (450 kg) of vegetables, donated to food banks and shelters because Via Verde residents had not yet moved in. GrowNYC also works closely with Via Verde's garden club members and conducts workshops on planting, harvesting, and composting. Membership is limited to 30—one-third are tenants and two-thirds are co-op owners. Rather than giving residents individual garden plots, Via Verde management followed the community garden model, in which the gardens are operated collectively. Garden club members select the vegetables and herbs each season and assign tasks to different members.

An important goal of Via Verde's urban agriculture program is to educate families about food production and healthy eating. Local chefs donate their time to lead cooking classes teaching Via Verde residents how to use seasonal produce from the gardens to prepare nutritious meals. GrowNYC also organizes a "food box" program, open to all residents: farmers set up a produce tent each Wednesday and charge $10 for 12 pounds (5.4 kg) of seasonal fruits and vegetables. Residents who receive federal nutrition assistance get a $2 discount.

Max Ruperti, senior property manager with Phipps Houses, who oversees operations at Via Verde, estimates that 1 to 2 percent of the development's operating budget is devoted to maintaining the gardens and green roofs. The plan is to gradually shift stewardship of the community garden from GrowNYC to residents. In this third year, GrowNYC's contract for garden services is significantly smaller than in previous years, and as residents assume greater responsibility for the garden, operating costs will shrink. Ruperti notes unanticipated added costs: pest control

associated with organic gardening and higher water costs during dry summers.

Education and communication are key to a successful urban agriculture program. "We felt the residents needed guidance in the first couple of years, so we hired GrowNYC to start the gardens. Now they act as mentors to the garden club members," says Ruperti. Ruperti waited to start the club until residents were taught the responsibilities associated with membership. The garden club membership application contains explicit rules—for example, committing members to at least three hours of work per week during gardening season and participation in at least six of eight monthly garden and cooking workshops. Likewise, garden rules—prohibition of smoking, eating, drinking, and playing music—are clearly communicated to residents when they move in.

Performance

Units were absorbed quickly. The 151 rental units, offered through a lottery, attracted 7,000 applications; 5,000 people are on a waiting list. The for-sale units sold out in seven months. Intended as a new model for urban housing, Via Verde demonstrates a commitment to create the next generation of housing that addresses poverty, health, and sustainability. The development has won national recognition and received numerous awards from local and national organizations, such as the American Planning Association, the Urban Land Institute, and the New York chapters of the American Society of Landscape Architects and the American Institute of Architects.

Brightly colored, prominent, and well-lit staircases encourage residents to walk instead of taking the elevators.
Robert Garneau

Grow Community
Bainbridge Island, Washington

PROJECT DATA

USE
MASTER-PLANNED COMMUNITY
24 SINGLE-FAMILY HOMES AND
20 MULTIFAMILY UNITS IN PHASE I;
132 RESIDENCES AT BUILDOUT

YEAR OPENED
2013

SITE SIZE
8 AC (3.2 HA)

RENTAL RATES/SALES PRICES
APARTMENTS: $1.75–$1.95 PER
SQ FT
HOMES: $295,000–$525,000,
DEPENDING ON LOCATION AND
FLOOR PLAN—1,180–1,880 SQ FT
(110–175 SQ M)

PROJECT COST
PHASE I: $16 MILLION, INCLUDING
LAND

DEVELOPER/OWNER
ASANI DEVELOPMENT

ARCHITECTS
DAVIS STUDIO ARCHITECTURE +
DESIGN LLC, CUTLER
ANDERSON ARCHITECTS

LENDER
BUILDERS CAPITAL

EQUITY PARTNERS
A GROUP OF FIVE INDIVIDUAL
LOCAL INVESTORS

"EVERY ELEMENT OF GROW COMMUNITY is intentionally planned to create a sense of community. The physical structure as well as community programs are designed to build an interactive environment and strong social network for people to form close connections with their neighbors," says Marja Preston, president of Asani Development, the project developer. The developer chose to follow the One Planet Living framework; Grow Community is one of only seven endorsed One Planet Communities in the world. The principles of One Planet promote zero-carbon buildings, a reduction in water use, waste reduction, and use of sustainable, healthy building materials. But they also call for "encouraging active, sociable, meaningful lives to promote good health and well-being"—the primary tenet that shaped the design of Grow Community. The developer chose to follow the One Planet principles with the goal of creating a profitable, and therefore replicable, development model. An important element of this strategy was to provide housing at a price point that young families, single households, and individuals on fixed incomes could afford.

Grow Community was designed to encourage walking, biking, and engagement with neighbors.
Deb Henderson

Phase I of this three-phase residential community combines 24 single-family homes with 20 rental apartments organized around shared community gardens. At buildout, the eight-acre (3.2 ha) development will have 132 residences, a community center, and an early childhood center.

Main Wellness Features

CHEMICAL-FREE INDOORS

Following the One Planet Communities guidelines, the zero-net-carbon homes at Grow Community are constructed with sustainable healthy materials that contain no harmful chemicals and emit no noxious fumes. Preston notes that homes built at a similar price point to that of Grow Community typically have vinyl windows, which do not meet One Planet goals. Asani decided to use wood/fiberglass windows to meet the sustainable materials guidelines, even though this option resulted in a 25 percent cost increase for the overall window package. The result is a home with more durable, longer-lasting windows and better indoor air quality.

DESIGN FOR PEDESTRIANS AND BICYCLISTS

The site, on the edge of the town of Winslow on Bainbridge Island, is a five-minute walk from city hall, the local farmers market, and shops, and ten minutes from the ferry terminal, which is a short ride from downtown Seattle. Its Walk Score of 80 confirms that it is in a "very walkable" location.

On-site strategies to promote walking and exercise are the following:

* Parking in Phase I is on the perimeter of the site; residents use paths crossing through the community gardens to reach their homes on foot. This design, derived from focus-group participants, was intended to encourage walking and biking and spontaneous encounters with neighbors, and to encourage people to think twice before driving. Preston notes that from an urban planning perspective, perimeter parking is an interesting concept, but seems risky to developers and investors. Nonetheless, Asani decided to follow prospective residents' recommendations in Phase I.

The paths were designed to be safe and inviting for both adults and children. Vehicle roads are separated so cars never cross the walking paths. In place of playgrounds inserted in the community, the paths were designed with natural play elements, such as circles of flat granite rock for children to jump on and play on. The site was designed so that parents would feel comfortable letting their children walk on their-

design components where they could remain into old age. By placing parking beneath the buildings in Phase II, the design not only eliminates the visual impact of surface parking and minimizes impervious area, but it also allows three of the five acres in the second phase to be used for open space and community gardens.

＊ To further reduce the amount of car use, thereby encouraging walking, the developer started a car-share program: residents pay a small monthly fee to use a Nissan Leaf car. The charging station for the car is connected to a dedicated solar array that provides sufficient renewable energy to power the car.

COMMUNITY GARDENS/SOCIAL INTERACTION

Instead of having individual front yards, the single-family homes are clustered around community gardens. In Phase I, the first of four gardens (one per pocket neighborhood) was constructed for the model homes built in 2012. Asani plans to hold "work parties" to help residents build their gardens and to build a sense of community. Asani will provide soil and other materials for these early gardens before they are turned over to residents. In order to share resources and expertise, residents decided recently to manage all four garden spaces as one large "urban farm" rather than allocate separate plots to each household.

A nonprofit organization, Grow:Connected, will manage programs for the community center. The

Garages are not part of the first phase, so storage sheds and shared bike barns are provided for residents. *Deb Henderson*

own to town, where the library, schools, and the swimming pool are only minutes away.

＊ Because there are no garages, the homes have storage sheds for bicycles, garden tools, and other outdoor gear. A number of residents have too many bikes to fit in the shed (one resident owns eight), so the developer built additional shared bike barns and storage for kayaks. Later phases, however, will have parking underground in response to input from baby boomers, whose interest in Grow Community was not anticipated by the developer. These older prospective residents also wanted one-story homes with universal

Interiors of Grow Community homes feature chemical-free materials and wood-frame windows. *Anthony Rich*

developer envisions creating an "eco-concierge" position within the nonprofit. The concierge would develop educational programs about urban gardening, One Planet Living, green building, and renewable energy.

Preston notes the importance of meeting early with potential residents to learn their preferences. Another bit of information gleaned from these early meetings was a strong preference for intergenerational living: potential residents 55 and older showed a strong desire to live in a community with families and children. Asani plans to design the daycare center with universal design elements to accommodate older residents for volunteer work with children.

Performance

With no comparable residential projects in the region that lenders could consider when weighing a loan, Asani Development, made up of a group of local investors, put up the equity itself for the three model for-sale homes. When Grow Community opened in August 2012, Seattle's housing market was still sluggish, so Asani expected lackluster

sales. Instead, the first 22 for-sale units on the market sold out within six months. There is a long waiting list for rental units still under construction; current rental units go for $1.75–$1.95 per square foot, while other rental properties have typically gone for $1.10–$1.25 per square foot. Sales were so strong that Asani had to accelerate its construction schedule. "We're halfway through construction on Phase I, in schematics for Phase II, and people already want to reserve units in Phase III," notes Preston. "We intended to list on the MLS, but haven't needed to." Although advertising did not extend beyond Bainbridge Island, only half the residents came from the island; the rest came from around the United States and Canada.

Four community gardening spaces provide residents with opportunities to grow their own produce and to build a sense of community.
Deb Henderson

Selandra Rise
Casey, Australia

IN 2008, THE STATE GOVERNMENT OF VICTORIA and the Planning Institute of Australia launched a groundbreaking partnership to facilitate a blueprint for residential greenfield development projects. Stockland, Australia's largest residential developer, joined this partnership to create Selandra Rise, a demonstration project focused on principles of health and well-being, as well

Selandra Community Place holds 20 to 30 monthly community programs.
Stockland

as diverse and affordable housing options and employment opportunities within the project. Selandra Rise delivered a variety of programs, amenities, and housing price points previously not available in the Melbourne market, says Mike Davis, Stockland's general manager of residential development.

Selandra Rise is a 115-hectare (284 ac) master-planned community in the city of Casey, 50 kilometers (30 mi) south of Melbourne. The community currently has 65 townhouses and 793 two-, three-, four-, and five-bedroom single-family detached homes. The first phase opened to residents in 2011, and the development is progressively being built out with input from the residents as the community grows and evolves.

Main Wellness Features

Even with the focus on health-promoting features, Selandra Rise cost no more than comparable projects Stockland has developed, Davis says. However, the company did have to commit a great deal of time to ensure that the community was delivered as envisioned by the partners. The cost of the wellness components was only 1 to 2 percent of the total project cost, he estimates. The project was funded from Stockland's balance sheet, with no equity partners needed at the table. The partnership aspect of Selandra Rise has benefited Stockland from both a development and an operations standpoint. Stockland built much of the community infrastructure, but partners—including the city of Casey, the Victorian Health Promotion Foundation (VicHealth), and the Growth Areas Authority (representing the Victoria state government)—brought many services to the table as well.

Hilltop Park includes outdoor fitness equipment.
Stockland

An off-street biking and walking path is located along Clyde Creek.
Stockland

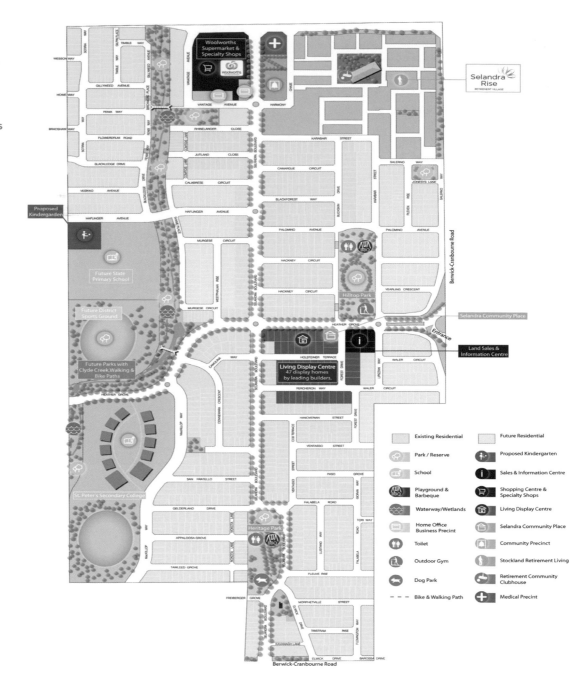

RESIDENTIAL PROXIMITY TO PARKS AND COMMUNITY WELLNESS FACILITIES

All homes are within 300 meters (less than a quarter mile) of parkland, giving residents easy access by foot or bike to the Clyde Creek trail, small pocket parks, and larger destination parks that contain facilities such as playgrounds.

Hilltop Park, centrally located within the development, has an outdoor fitness station with a variety of exercise machines similar to what would be found in an indoor gym. A sports park is also planned for a later phase. Heritage Park, opened in March 2014, incorporates a community garden that was planned and designed by the residents.

DESIGN FOR PEDESTRIANS AND BICYCLISTS

Walkability within Selandra Rise was a key development principle pursued by Stockland and its partners. The community was designed to have a permeable and gridded street network that ensures direct connections among residences, open space, and community facilities, with short blocks and sidewalks lined with trees.

The street network and the off-street path network encourage walking and biking. A wayfinding system informs residents of the time it will take them to walk and bike to various destinations within the community. In addition to the dedicated bike lanes and sidewalks that line the streets of the development, two kilometers (1.25 mi) of wide off-street walking and bike paths are located along Clyde Creek and in Hilltop and Heritage parks.

WELLNESS PROGRAMMING AND SOCIAL INTERACTION

Selandra Community Place (SCP), a community facility operated by the city of Casey and centrally located within the Selandra Rise development, opened shortly after the first community's residents moved in. SCP organizes and promotes health, wellness, and social activities for residents. Twenty to 30 programs per month are arranged by SCP, including walking groups both for children going to and from school and for adults, allowing them to socialize; food-sharing programs; cooking and gardening lessons; and fitness classes. The free programs are tailored to the needs of the community, with classes added or dropped based on those needs. In addition to providing opportunities for improving physical health, SCP programming helps promote the social cohesion of the new community, offering residents the opportunity to meet their neighbors and reinforcing safety.

SCP also acts as a laboratory for sustainable and healthy building design, showcasing elements that residents can emulate, such as use of healthy building materials and strategies for improving indoor air quality.

Performance

The market response to Selandra Rise has been extremely favorable. According to Davis, it is the fastest-selling community project in Australia. Home prices range from A$295,000 to A$595,000 (with an average price of A$370,000)—A$7,000 to A$12,000 higher than competitor projects. The higher prices and sales volumes are linked directly with the health and wellness focus of the project, Davis says. "In time, I expect that the things embedded at Selandra Rise will become an expectation in the marketplace," he says.

Operating expenses are similar to those of other Stockland projects, even with the specialized health and wellness components. Partners such as

the city of Casey are primarily responsible for the programming costs.

The partnership component of Selandra Rise was different from that of the typical Stockland developments, but provided the opportunity to create a dynamic and successful new community. In addition, Stockland learned about the importance of articulating specific marketing messages to potential residents through open discussions of the importance of health and well-being. Davis says the Selandra Rise process has offered many insights that will have benefits across Stockland's entire portfolio as a range of new projects integrate similar livability principles.

Studies

An especially innovative aspect of this development is a multiyear longitudinal study of the community, funded by project partner VicHealth, which will produce quantitative data on how the range of wellness initiatives benefits residents. The study has begun, with the first 18 to 24 months of data collection establishing the baseline for the residents. Stockland will be evaluating the baseline and how the community evolves in order to ensure that Selandra Rise is contributing to the community's health and well-being, and will make programming or infrastructure adjustments if results are not as expected.

Residents have played a role in the design of the community's open spaces.
Stockland

Rancho Sahuarita
Tucson, Arizona

INSPIRED BY SOME OF THE COUNTRY'S GREAT master-planned communities—such as Columbia, Maryland; Reston, Virginia; Celebration, Florida; and Rancho Mission Viejo, California—developer Robert Sharpe set out to create the most affordable, highly amenitized, lifestyle-oriented community in southern Arizona founded on promoting physical, social, and emotional well-being. By making physical activity and other elements of wellness readily accessible, the developer made it easier for residents to pursue healthy life choices. Moreover, convenience and easy access to these health-related amenities were important in appealing to the community's primary market— first-time buyers and generation X families—as well as in distinguishing Rancho Sahuarita from competing neighborhoods.

A safari trail with life-size bronze animals is one of the kid-friendly community features that encourage play. *Rancho Sahuarita*

Located nine miles (14.5 km) south of Tucson in the town of Sahuarita, Rancho Sahuarita, is a 3,000-acre (1,200 ha) master-planned community with a town center and a central Lake Park. Since 2002, national homebuilders have sold more than 5,000 homes—about half of the residential portion of the project—and there are currently more than 15,000 residents.

Main Wellness Features

AMENITIES FOR PHYSICAL AND SOCIAL ACTIVITY

The developer has invested more than $100 million in community infrastructure, with about 30 percent allocated to amenities that encourage healthy physical and social activities.

To help offset the cost of this extensive amenities package, Rancho Sahuarita assesses a "parks and rec" fee of $2,500 per home on builders and the HOA charges a 1 percent "community enhancement fee" on resale houses. The HOA's annual operating budget, which is funded by monthly dues of $93 per home, is about $5.5 million, with about 40 percent of this income spent on maintenance of the amenities.

✳ **Ten-acre lake as community focus.** When Sharpe created the ten-acre (4 ha) Sahuarita

Lake, he set back homes from the water to provide space for a park and a wide pedestrian promenade. Lake Park, which is visible from two collector roads, serves the entire community and is a popular venue for concerts, art fairs, triathlons, parades, and festivals.

✳ **Community facilities.** The Rancho Sahuarita Clubhouse, a 30,000-square-foot (2,800 sq m) recreational facility located on the lake, has a 6,000-square-foot (560 sq m) fitness center with cardiovascular and strength-training equipment, dance and aerobic studios, multipurpose rooms, a lap pool, and a splash park. Residents can select from more than 50 classes a week, most of which are covered by the HOA fee, including karate, yoga, ballet, tennis, and stability ball classes; residents can register online for events and classes. Personal training and sports camps are also offered, and a fee is charged for some of the more advanced programs.

The clubhouse also has an "adventure park" with an activities lawn, basketball and tennis courts, a playground, and a mini-golf course. Sharpe's goal is to use Rancho Sahuarita's facilities and services to help busy generation X households pursue a healthy lifestyle as they take care of ordinary chores and responsibilities. For example, Rancho Sahuarita's on-site baby-sitting service makes it easy and convenient

for residents to work out at the health club or swim at the pool without having to worry about taking care of their kids.

* **Neighborhood facilities.** Neighborhoods are served by 15 pocket parks and several larger satellite parks with pools, volleyball and basketball courts, and other amenities to promote physical activity.
* **Kid-friendly community facilities.** The developer created butterfly and desert gardens for children, as well as an African animal safari trail, replete with life-size animals in bronze.
* **Paths and trails.** Forty miles (64 km) of paved walking paths and bicycle trails connect residents to schools, parks, and commercial and recreational areas.

PARTNERSHIPS TO PROMOTE FITNESS AND HEALTH

The developer's primary strategy for promoting health care and wellness is to form partnerships with like-minded stakeholders such as Carondelet Health Network, a major health care provider in the Tucson area, which operates a primary and urgent-care facility in Rancho Sahuarita's Marketplace shopping center. Carondelet is in the design phase for a larger Health and Wellness Pavilion in the community's town center, which will combine on-site urgent care with preventative health care facilities.

Rancho Sahuarita also partners with Carondelet to offer a children's "Be Well" Summer Camp, a "Healthier You" lecture series, a Health and Wellness Day, and "Walk with a Doc" and "Lunch and Learn" programs that provide residents the opportunity to ask local physicians questions. In addition, Carondelet supports Rancho Sahuarita's kindness program by giving a "kindness mug" to residents at coffee socials to encourage compassion and empathy in the community. This emphasis on the relationship among kindness, happiness, and mental health furthers Rancho Sahuarita's goal of creating a friendly place to live in by promoting kindness as a key to emotional and social well-being.

The developer has partnered with numerous other organizations—United Way of Tucson and Southern

Top: The ten-acre (4 ha) lake is a popular venue for community-wide events. *Rancho Sahuarita*

Center: Among the activities organized by the community are sports camps for kids. *Rancho Sahuarita*

Bottom: The splash park and lap pool are popular for fun and fitness in the Arizona heat. *Rancho Sahuarita*

Arizona, American Red Cross, United Community Health, Tucson Alliance for Autism, and the Young Athletes program of the Special Olympics—to enhance health and wellness programming.

Rancho Sahuarita also has a strong working relationship with the Sahuarita Unified School District (SUSD), which has located six of its schools and recreational amenities in the community and within walking distance of most of the homes. The development's "walking school bus" provides parents and children the opportunity to exercise together every day. SUSD's health-related summer activities include free baseball camps and swimming programs at the new aquatic center located in the town center.

Sharpe notes that in response to the recession, many developers have elected to cut costs and have incorporated lower-budget amenity approaches into their master-planned communities, like programmed open space. He emphasizes the importance of investing in hard infrastructure—such as the activity center, the lake, parks, and linear parks with walkways—that creates venues for the "soft" programming. "Programming is not a quick, easy, and inexpensive solution to create instant community," adds Sharpe's son Jeremy, who heads Rancho Sahuarita's community development endeavors. "It requires enormous effort and commitment to do programming well."

Performance

Since 2002, national homebuilders have sold more than 5,000 homes at Rancho Sahuarita with a total value topping $1 billion, making the development one of the best-selling master-planned communities in the country. Rancho Sahuarita has continually dominated southern Arizona's housing market, accounting for an 8 to 18 percent share of sales in the Tucson metro area.

From 2001 to 2006, it's platted lot prices more than doubled. During the same period, Rancho Sahuarita's home prices, which initially experienced a 10 percent discount to similar homes in better-located subdivisions, rose almost 80 percent and now command a 10 percent premium. Robert Sharpe attributes these price increases and the accelerated sales pace to Rancho Sahuarita's healthy lifestyle, amenities, and programming. "Our overall success indicates that the strategic positioning of a development through an amenities program that promotes health and wellness can differentiate a community from competing neighborhoods and mitigate long-term risks," he says.

Forty miles (64 km) of paved paths connect residents to schools, parks, and commercial and recreational areas.
Rancho Sahuarita

Mueller
Austin, Texas

PROJECT DATA

USE
MASTER-PLANNED COMMUNITY
5,700 HOMES AT BUILDOUT, 25
PERCENT AFFORDABLE

OTHER USES
4 MILLION SQ FT (372,000 SQ M)
RETAIL AND OFFICE

YEAR OPENED
2007

SITE SIZE
700 AC (283 HA)

SALES PRICES/RENTAL RATES
MARKET-RATE SALES: $150,000–
$1,000,000

AFFORDABLE HOME SALES:
$125,000–$210,000

MARKET-RATE RENTALS:
$879–$3,860

PROJECT COST
$300 MILLION

DEVELOPER/OWNER
CATELLUS, CITY OF AUSTIN (JOINT
PROJECT)

MASTER PLAN/URBAN DESIGN
ROMA DESIGN GROUP, MCCANN
ADAMS STUDIO

FINANCING
The city of Austin owns and holds
the land until it is taken down
for infrastructure or vertical
development. Catellus funds all the
infrastructure costs with its own
equity and is reimbursed for public
infrastructure through tax increment
financing or land sales revenue.

MUELLER WAS DESIGNED TO BE AUSTIN'S MODEL of antisprawl and sustainable development. However, as it has evolved, certain principles of sustainability were implemented in ways now recognized as promoting community health and wellness, including protection of air quality, increased pedestrian activity, and use of low-emission building materials.

Mueller's 700-acre (283 ha) site is at the former municipal airport just three miles (4.8 km) from downtown Austin and two miles (3.2 km) from the University of Texas. The first phase opened in 2007 with 350 single-family and 442 multifamily homes and 240,000 square feet (22,300 sq m) of retail space.

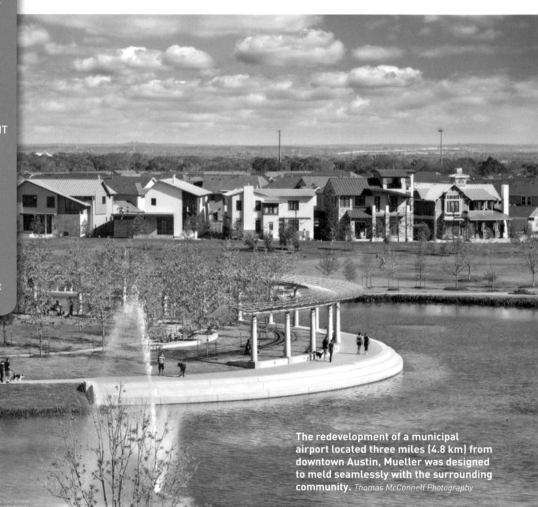

The redevelopment of a municipal airport located three miles (4.8 km) from downtown Austin, Mueller was designed to meld seamlessly with the surrounding community. *Thomas McConnell Photography*

Currently there are 1,970 homes, 1.8 million square feet (167,000 square m) of retail and office space, and 75 acres (30 ha) of parks, with 3,500 residents and 3,500 employees. At buildout, projected for 2020, Mueller will have more than 5,700 homes, 25 percent of which will be reserved for low-income households; 4 million square feet (372,000 sq m) of commercial and office space; and 140 acres (57 ha) of public parks and open space. Mueller is well on the way to achieving its grand vision of melting seamlessly into the rest of the city.

Main Wellness Features

COMPREHENSIVE NETWORK OF OPEN SPACE AND STREETS

Master developer Catellus Development Corporation and master planners ROMA Design and McCann Adams Studio worked to develop complete streets and open-space networks within Mueller that include the following:

* Sidewalks with shade trees that provide pedestrian comfort during the extreme Texas heat and connect to a comprehensive trail system—important for both recreation and the residents' ability to move around the community—to further encourage walking and cycling. This trail system links to existing parks and open space outside the site, extending access to recreation for Mueller residents, as well as allowing residents of the surrounding community—who played a role in creating a vision for the site—to be connected to the new parks, amenities, and retail space at Mueller.

* A network of protected bike lanes—provided in an update of the original master plan—that are buffered from automobile traffic by concrete curbing. Existing streets have been retrofitted with the improved safety measures, and new streets planned for future phases will incorporate these cycle tracks.
* Recreation features such as sports courts, a state-of-the-art children's playground, and a stretching area with pull-up bars and outdoor showers at Lake Park. Community gardens and a working orchard are planned in future phases at Mueller.

SOCIAL INTERACTION

Before opening the first phase of Mueller, Catellus organized a block party to help new residents meet their neighbors and share contact information before moving into their homes. This forging of social connections early on led to formation of grassroots interest-based groups, in addition to the community's property owner's association, shortly after residents moved in. Residents have formed more than 40 different clubs, including fitness clubs. "There is so much community activity, we as a developer could never keep up with it all," says Deanne Desjardin, vice president of Mueller marketing. External organizations organize events in Mueller's open spaces as well; Lake Park alone draws more than 70,000 people per year to larger-scale events.

The design of the residences in Mueller also facilitates social contact: homes are constructed with front porches to encourage interaction between residents and their neighbors out walking

Most homes include porches to encourage social interaction between neighbors.
Thomas McConnell Photography

A network of trails and sidewalks promotes biking and walking.
Thomas McConnell Photography (top)
Holly Reed Photography (bottom)

and cycling. This interaction is also encouraged by the location of the homes on each lot. The homes are located very close to the sidewalks with small front yards, facilitated by midblock alleys that move the garages to the back of the homes. These alleys also provide additional outdoor spaces for play and gathering.

CLEAN INDOOR AIR

All homes and commercial buildings in Mueller are required to be built to city of Austin Energy Green Building standards, which emphasize a healthy indoor environment. At all its Mueller residences, David Weekley Homes, one of the larger home-builders in the community, uses healthy, low-toxin building materials, a tight building envelope, and controlled and filtered mechanical ventilation systems that bring in fresh air. Jim Rado, area president for David Weekley Homes, estimates that the firm spends an average of $2 to $3 per square foot to ensure healthy indoor air along with upgraded energy efficiency products in all homes across its portfolio, but has seen good returns on that investment.

Performance

More than 1,000 people signed up for a lottery for Phase I lots when homebuilders only had sketches to show, and the 350 Phase I homes sold out.

About ten different builders have designed and constructed homes at Mueller; David Weekley

Homes has built 35 to 40 percent of all units and over 60 percent of the affordable units—both townhouses and single-family homes—to date. Rado and Ken Swisher, division president of David Weekley Homes, note that absorption rates in Mueller are the highest of any community they are building in, and at the highest price per foot. There are a variety of factors unique to the development have contributed to this success. Though the healthy features at Mueller play a role in this success, so do other factors, such as proximity to downtown; the architectural style of the homes (unique in Austin due to strict Mueller guidelines); and the strength of Catellus's master plan.

Though Catellus says breaking out the development and operations costs of the wellness components from the total project cost is difficult, it acknowledges that these components have added cost to development while also contributing to the project's success. The project team has no doubt that Mueller's wellness components attracted res-

idents and increased the marketability of commercial sites to prospective office developers, as well. According to Jim Adams, former principal at ROMA Design and current principal of McCann Adams Design Studio, some residents waited for specific lots that would put them close to a park, a trail, or the grocery store.

Studies

Studies by the University of Texas and Texas A&M have examined the effects of the pedestrian and bicycle orientation of Mueller on resident's activity levels. In both studies, residents reported they had increased their physical activity—walking and biking—by 40 to 50 minutes per week. Catellus is currently providing development information to other studies measuring health-related variables such as physical activity and access to healthy food in order to better understand their effects on resident health.

All of Mueller's homes and commercial buildings are built to the city of Austin's Green Building standards.
Thomas McConnell Photography